MERA BHARAT MAHAN

M.G. Vaidya

Published by
PRABHAT PRAKASHAN PVT. LTD.
4/19 Asaf Ali Road,
New Delhi-110 002 (INDIA)
e-mail: prabhatbooks@gmail.com

ISBN 978-93-5266-143-5
MERA BHARAT MAHAN
by Shri M.G. Vaidya

Translator
Dr. Balram Misra

Edition
2025

Price
₹ 400.00 (Rupees Four Hundred only)

Printed at
Narula Printers, Delhi

MERA
BHARAT MAHAN

PREFACE

It is quite often that we read various catchphrases written on the rear of a truck. Quite often, I read and relish the words. Once I read such a catchphrase in Hindi: "Sau me se ninyanabe be-iman, phir bhi mera Bharat mahan." It means that ninety-nine out of one hundred Indians are dishonest, still my India is great. For a moment, I laughed at the comment, and then I became a little introspective. A question flashed in my mind: *Is the number of persons who make India great so insignificant*? As a matter of fact, there are so many persons engaged silently in the process of service for making India a great nation. They shun limelight, keep away from publicity, and live only to preoccupy their life in unnoticed service for others, so I wrote about such persons. This book is the compilation of articles about such persons only.

—M.G. Vaidya

TRANSLATOR'S NOTE

Progress with efforts to be great, greater greatest; is a natural instinct of a living person, a living society, and a living nation. No doubt, attainments of desirable objectives like cleanliness, efficiency, prosperity, safety, supreme military power, vibrant economy, national and international awards – like The Nobel and Olympic, annual growth of GDP, democracy, social justice, honesty and competence of the people and leaders, are taken as indicators of greatness, but their value assumes greater dimensions and importance if these objectives are attained through voluntary contributions, without any exterior pressure of fear or temptation. Even a negligible contribution matters, as was evidenced by the legendary squirrel's devoted role in the construction of the *Ram-Setu*. What is greatness? A proverb quoted in this book by the author, Shri M.G. Vaidya, says, "Greatness lies not in owning resources, power, status or prestige. It lies in politeness, gentle demeanour, service and strength of character. Greatness is not in being powerful; it is in right application of power." Readers will be happy to find that with this standard of greatness all the common looking characters of this book are great, and, that is how they make India a great nation.

Selfless service, not driven by selfish commercial and political motives, has always been the very core and distinct hallmark of the Indian culture and ethos. This hoary tradition has been illustrated poetically in the following Sanskrit adage:

> *"Pibanti nadyah swayameva nodakam,*
> *Swayam na khaadanti phalaani vrukshaah,*
> *Naadanti sasyam khalu vaarivaahaah,*
> *Paropakaaraaya sataam vibhutayah."*
> (पिबन्ति नद्यः स्वयमेव नोदकं, स्वयं न खादन्ति फलानि वृक्षाः
> नादंति सस्यं खलु वारिवाहाः, परोपकाराय सतां विभूतयः)

The adage says that rivers do not drink their water themselves. Trees do not eat their fruits themselves. Clouds themselves do not eat cereals produced by the crops irrigated by their water. Great and gentle persons live their life for others. It is the spirit of this unique message of social service that seems to have motivated the characters of this book. True to their traditional ethos, they served society silently, shunning limelight.

In the year 2000, when I was transferred from the Media Cell of the BJP Central Office, Delhi, to work in and subsequently take over as the chief of the R.S.S. Media Centre, Delhi, called Indraprasth Vishwa Samvad Kendra, my revered friend Devendra Swarup ji, the well-known columnist, former editor of Hindi weekly *Panchajanya,* and a historian, asked me to be in touch with Shri M.G. Vaidya who had come from Nagpur to Delhi to work as R.S.S. Spokesman. Vaidya ji needed an assistant in his staff, so I was deputed to assist him. Contrary to his reputation of being a stern scholar, I found in him abundant simplicity imbued with purposiveness. I noted that one of his prime concerns was the unjust and irresponsible stand taken by a section of the media against the R.S.S. The way the post-Independence Indian media allowed its own degeneration to pure professionalism from its missionary and dedicated commitment of the pre-Independence era has been an issue of deep concern for Shri Vaidya. His observations and un-minced sharp comments on the mischievous omissions and commissions by some editors, their negative, cunning and subtle nuances in most of the editorial notes about R.S.S., and, indeed, everything native, and some TV channels, unsettled many men and women of both, print and visual media. His *'Angad-Pad'* humbled many of them, and some of the adamant ones had to face judicial defeat; in due course apologizing, some in writing. A well-known English daily of Delhi had to publish an apology to the Sangh on its front page. His frequent press conferences created a stir in most of the media houses. They were convinced that the R.S.S. Spokesman had a vision to share with the media people. A renowned Delhi-based English daily invited him to address its editorial team. He went there and interacted with the learned editorial staff, but criticized vehemently the editorial notes of some of the newspapers for becoming *'advertorial notes'*. Almost all media houses, except a prominent English daily of Chennai, appreciated the R.S.S. Spokesman's views on highlighting pro-India and positive news. The Chennai-based daily was adamant to stick to its undeclared editorial policy of playing to the tunes of anti-R.S.S. and anti-India elements. Once it published an article that aimed at palliating the incidents of terrorism in India. Vaidya ji wrote a letter to the editor in response to that damaging article. That letter was not published. As his assistant, I called that newspaper more than ten times to know from the editor why the letter was not published. Every time I had to hear terse remarks that meant the editor's refusal to speak to me on the subject. Pestered by my repeated telephonic calls, the lady P.A. to the editor kindly gave me the telephone number of the dealing sub-editor and asked me to speak to him. I spoke to him. Very gently the dealing sub-editor told me, "Sorry, we cannot publish Mr. Vaidya's letter as it is against our editorial policy, and no further discussion please", and the line was disconnected.

Delhi-based Hindi daily *Punjab Kesari* once published a piece that was offensive to the R.S.S. When I put up the concerned newspaper cutting to Vaidya ji, he was a little upset. He asked me to fix a meeting with the editor. I spoke to the editor, Shri Ashwini Kumar, and next day he welcomed us in his office. Vaidya ji's riposte humbled and convinced the learned editor, and his comments were published in his newspaper the same week. On knowing about Shri Vaidya's earlier career in journalism, the editor requested him to write a column for the *Punjab Kesari,* which he agreed to do. On our way back to our office, we saw a truck with the saying, "Sau me se ninyanabe beiman, phir bhi mera Bharat mahan!" ('Ninetynine out of one hundred Indians are dishonest, still my India is great!'). Vaidya ji became pensive and at length commented, '*Is the number of persons who make India great so small*?' Next day his article was ready for dispatch to *Punjab Kesari* for publication as the first piece of his column. The series of forty-three of his write ups was subsequently compiled and published by Lokhit Prakashan, Lucknow, as a book titled *Mera Bharat Mahan.*

Each article of the book is unique in its message of greatness, the message of self-less and inborn inspiration to serve others. It contains brief descriptions of how a poor Kishabhau Patvardhan created an institution called 'Swaroop Vardhini' to look after children of neglected habitations; how a Bhaiya ji Kane joined Manipur with Maharashtra; how a Girish Prabhune worked to ameliorate the lot of the nomadic tribes; how selflessly a Thakre Maharaj awakened society through *Varakari Kirtan*; how R.S.S. *pracharaks* like Brahma Deva and Chamanlal renounced careerism for the sake of service to the Motherland; how a new awakening took place in North-East; how Hindus of Maraad set right the distorted mentality of a few fundamentalist Muslims;

how selflessly Dr. Vasant Rao Tare served society; how Dr. Paralkar earned the title of *Friend of the Sick;* how a financially poor and illiterate Shankar Papalkar created a center of education for the hearing and speech impaired children of a primitive locality; how a self-less Ram Krishna Goswami tried to reform the life of prisoners through the *Gita;* how the Vidya Bharati has been geared up to improve the quality of our education system and how Vasant Rao Shevde served *Devi Saraswati.* It contains sagas of inborn and courageous initiative marshalled by Mangala, a Dalit woman village-head; an adamant bureaucrat named Rajnish Dube; a prodigy called Subramanian Chandrashekhara; an editor named Prakash Pohare; an Army officer named Lieutenant General Arjun Rai; the village women who raised a bank for women; the *Sewa Bharti*, which has been exerting silently to ensure social harmony through *Sewa* and *Sanskar*; Surendra Singh Chauhan, who created an ideal village; an MLA named Mahendra Mashru; a social worker named Frikshon Lingdoh; the heroic and silent services done by the Vanvasi Kalyan Ashram in primitive areas; the unique creation of Ocean of Bliss in Shegaon; story of development in Dhagevadi; and Chait Ram of Baripada, who was instrumental in transforming his backward and poor village into a prosperous area.

A very important point about this book is that it is a small glimpse of a part of the past; about life and activities of great characters as described by Shri M.G. Vaidya in the year 2002-03. So, it is natural for readers to be inquisitive about the present progress of the great men and women in question and their works. What were the factors that motivated their uniquely selfless social service, must be an interesting subject for study.

Mera Bharat Mahan in Hindi had been translated into Marathi and Punjabi languages also. I was present at the function that witnessed *Lokarpan* of the Punjabi edition at Jalandhar in April 2015. As desired by Shri Kishor Kant ji, the Punjab-*Prant pracharak* of R.S.S., I ventured to translate the book into English language.

Though I have put in my efforts, I seek indulgence of the readers to appreciate the fact that my capacity to import the original purports of the words of the common looking uncommon author to this translated work leaves a lot to be desired.

—Dr. Balram Misra

ACKNOWLEDGEMENTS

I express my gratitude to Maanneeya Shri M.G. Vaidya ji and Shri Dattatreya Hosabale, Maanneeya Sah Sarkayavah, for going through the draft translation, and suggesting me some important improvements. I fondly thank my grandson Angad Misra for helping me in typing My heartfelt gratitude to Smt. Aayushi Ketkar for giving the book a final shape before publication.

—Dr. Balram Misra

CONTENTS

Preface 5

Foreword 6

Translator's Note 7

Acknowledgements 13

1. Swaroop Vardhini 17
2. *'Nandan Van'* in Stones 21
3. From Manipur to Maharashtra 23
4. Girish Prabhune 27
5. Thakre Maharaj 31
6. Brahma dev 38
7. *'Nyishi'* Tribe 41
8. New *Vanaprasth Ashram* 45
9. Maraada: Attack and Counter Attack 49
10. Vasant Rao Tare 53
11. 'Rugna Mitra' (Friend of the Sick) 57
12. What is that Soil, Which Makes – Resolutely Assiduous and Courageous People? 61
13. World Veda Session 67
14. A Peculiar *'Sahyadri'* 70
15. Sewa Dham Vidya Mandir 76
16. Social Justice Court 80
17. *Niru* Lantern 82

18. Fragrance of Humanism 85
19. *Bhagavadgita* in Tihar Jail 90
20. Vidya Bharati 95
21. A Sage of Learning 100
22. International Cooperation Council 107
23. Jhansi ki Rani, and Her Tank 110
24. Mangala, A Dalit Sarpanch 113
25. Bank of Mothers' Milk 117
26. I.I.T. Kanpur Stunned the World of Science 119
27. Gift of Buddhism 122
28. Chennamma, The Queen of Kittur 127
29. Subramanian Chandrashekhara 131
30. Deshonnati 133
31. *Maan Bamaleshwari* Bank for Women 138
32. For Social Harmony 140
33. *Ganesh Poojan* in a Foreign Embassy 144
34. A Social Renaissance 146
35. *'Adarsh-Gram: Sanskar-Gram: Sanskrit-Gram'* 148
36. Want to meet the M.L.A.? Go to Hospital 152
37. Hospital in Siachen 154
38. Frikshon Lingdoh 157
39. Welcome Dawn of Desirable Change 160
40. 'Shegaon': An Ocean of Bliss 166
41. *'Dhagevadi'*: A Pilgrimage of Labour 172
42. *Chait Ram* of *Baripada* 176
43. Chamanlal 180

1

SWAROOP VARDHINI

"Swaroop Vardhini" or 'enhancer of one's own appearance'! What a beautiful name. Name and action are similar. There is no scarcity of unreal names. We say '*Soda Water*', but there is no soda in that. It is water without soda. The meaning of 'Swaroop Vardhini' is not like that. A thought came to my mind: Can appearance be enhanced and improved? It is given by God; but beauty-building is the invention of artists' talent. An artist changes the appearance of God-made stone, which then becomes a beautiful idol that is venerated. Is it possible in case of human beings? Can a human really change the appearance of other humans? The answer, naturally, is 'no'. Does the word human mean only human body? No, human being means human body with mind, conscience, sense, wit and even soul, for those who believe in soul. All these aspects have to be taken into account while defining a complete human being. Even though it may not be possible to bring change in the structure of human body, it is possible to change the mind, conscience, instincts and wit, etc. through a righteous process of purification and refinement, collectively meaning Sanskar. The Pune-based institute called "Swaroop Vardhini" is doing this very same work. Who runs this institute? Who envisioned such a beautiful name? It is Kishabhau Patvardhan. He lived for 81 years. He was recently awarded the 'P.P. Sri Guruji Puraskar'. Though technically he founded the

"Swaroop Vardhini" on May 13, 1979, the idea of the institute was born in his mind years before that.

Kishabhau paid a great deal of attention to children of backward classes of the society. In Pune, there is a backward locality called Mangalwar Peth. He surveyed the children of that locality. The survey revealed that about 50 percent children never went to school. The children who went to school in morning shifts never found their parents home when they came back at noon, as the parents, by then, had gone to work, and nobody was left behind to mind the children. They kept playing, doing mischiefs and getting into trouble. He directed his attention towards these children. He noted that many of the children were talented. That is how he decided to nurture their talents through his innovative institute called 'Swaroop Vardhini'. Kishabhau started enrolling to the Swaroop Vardhini the children who returned from their schools at noon and engaged them between 1:30 and 5 p.m. Apart from the school syllabus, he taught the children Sanskrit shlokas, Yogasanas, and innovative games with remarkable results.

The institute did not own any building. It had started working with 12 students in the shed of a factory in 1979. Today (in 2002) it is housed in its own grand building worth ₹ 45 lakh. The then *Sarsanghchalak* Shri Bala Sahab Deoras had inaugurated it in the year 1988. Just opposite it is a big slum population called 'Sadanand Nagar'. A *balwadi* (Child Welfare Centre) was started for the children of the slum. Ladies also came in contact through the *balwadi*. Tailoring and nursing classes were started for them. Adult literacy classes and camps for ladies also started. Legal counselling was made available to the ladies. That is how the process of "Swaroop Vardhan", the character makeup process, started. Now the social service outfits like *ajod* (incomparable), women's department, Arogya Kendra, Kutumb Salah

Kendra and various outfits of village development have affiliated themselves with the movement. Boys and girls from slum areas started studying, even in high schools. The students, who had no proper place and suitable atmosphere for study at their homes, started studying in the premises of "Swaroop Vardhini" at night from 9 to 12. About 250 students go there daily for study. While making available all necessary facilities for common students, Kishabhau paid extra attention to the superbly-talented children. For them, he made special efforts, and got suitable results. Dipak Dhampurkar, a student of the institute, scored first position in B.E. examination. Girish Adake got scholarship for Ph.D. As things stand today (year 2002), 400 students of Swaroop Vardhini. got admission in various outfits Now Swaroop Vardhini is not confined to Mangalwar Peth, other localities too have its branches. It succeeded in becoming a source of inspiration among students for social service. Three young girls named Dr. Manisha Boina, Ku. Pranjali Lakade and Ku. Rohini Tendulkar have gone to Arunachal to work for the Vanvasi Kalyan *Ashram*. Ku. Mangala and Ku. Kudalingar did social service in the terror-infested '*Bodo Pradesh*'.

Kishabhau was not a financially rich man. He was a R.S.S. *pracharak* from 1945 to 1951, and thereafter, he accepted the offer to work as a teacher in Dhanaraj Giraji School. Subsequently, he became Head Master and retired. After retirement, he did not spend his time in leisure. He spent his time in social service. The boys and girls he bonded with were not his caste fellows or relatives; still he spent his time with them.

In 2001, I attended a function organised by *Dr. Ambedkar Adhyayan Kendra*, Nagpur. There I raised a few questions: "There are many persons in our society who have attained high education, earned fortune and prestige because of the teachings of Dr. Ambedkar. Why is it that their attention does not reach the backward sections of their own community? Why do the teachers not run free classes for students of 10th-12th classes? Why do they not run centers for adult education? Why do they not hold camps to educate women? Virtually, education should expand and develop sympathy quite extensively and pervasively, enable one's consciousness to be generous, liberal and benevolent. It should enable one to intensify close affinity and brotherhood with others. Should education increase alienation or decrease it?" Perhaps my questions will be answered by Kishabhau's *Swaroop Vardhini*. It is noteworthy that Kishabhau had no intention of demanding votes for his services. He had no desire to contest any election.

□

"You have to grow from the inside out. None can teach you, none can make you spiritual. There is no other teacher but your own soul."

—Swami Vivekananda ji

2

'NANDAN VAN' IN STONES

Sachchidanand Bharti is now 45, but he had made up his mind to bring prosperity to his hills twenty years ago. Poudhi is the name of a district in the state of Uttaranchal. Ufraikhal is the name of a village in that district. This village and some other small hamlets jointly constitute a *Gram Sabha*, the village council. It is a stony region, where Sachchidanand undertook the task of making reservoirs for holding water, and plantation. About twenty years have elapsed since then. How many small pools could he have bound, and how many trees could he have planted? Seven thousand pools and 15 lakh trees. The whole area has become lush with greenery. Could one man named Sachchidanand Bharti have done all that alone? No. The initiative and impetus was provided by him, but he took along with him all the villagers. An institution named Lok Vikas Sangathan was founded. He belongs to village Dudha Toli. He convened a congregation of the villagers and explained to them the issues related with their common weal. While still a student, he came in contact with 'Chhatra Sangharsh Vahini' and the agitation led by Lok Nayak Jaya Prakash Narayan. It was that association which gifted to his personal life the effulgence and enthusiasm of the vision of public life, and his life course was transformed.

Shri Bharti chose his village Dudha Toli as the center of his social activities after earning his B.Ed. degree.

He had heard the name of Rajendra Singh of Alwar (Rajasthan), the winner of Magasaysay Award. Shri Bharti met him and decided to work in his stony region. Though there is a good amount of rain on hills, the whole rain water is drained out, so Bharti carved out small pools, which served as rainwater reservoirs. Plantations were done around these pools and the barren-stony land became lush green. Sachchidanand Bharti knows the art of organizing people. He exhorted the people to devote one day every month to worship the village deity and devote the remaining 29 days for routine household tasks. How the village deity is worshipped once a month? That day is devoted for cleaning village drains, plantation and maintaining streets. All the villagers get together and serve the village, unitedly, once a month. Solidarity among the people has changed the atmosphere of the village. The fame of Bharti's good work has spread around. Foreigners also visited his work site and appreciated it. They offered to donate money, but Bharti declined the offer saying that no financial help was required from government or foreign agencies. The reputation of this work affected the people of nearby areas. In 133 villages, the *Mahila Mangal Dal*, women welfare groups, were formed. These groups are active in the field of social reforms. How can sustainable prosperity and effort in work lag behind when women come forward? Shri K.S. Sudarshan ji, the then *Sar Sanghchalak*, visited Sachchidanand Bharti's social work sites. He was happy to see the work and stayed one whole day with him and enjoyed talking to villagers during night.

□

> *"Knowledge without good conduct of a person is as polluted as water kept in a skull and milk kept in a bag made of dog's skin. Contamination of a place of shelter pollutes the occupant."*
>
> —**Mahabharat**

3

FROM MANIPUR TO MAHARASHTRA

Chinchwad is the name of a city near Pune. *Chinch* is the Marathi version of tamarind. *Wad* is the Marathi version of banyan tree. Perhaps it was due to abundance of tamarind and banyan trees there that the place was called Chinchwad. Now it is a big city with Municipal Corporation. I am not going to write about that place. I am going to write about a function that was convened there on 1st of November 2001. It was the occasion of inauguration of a small boarding house and release of a biography. "*So what is special about it*?" Someone may ask this question. Boarding houses are built and inaugurated frequently. Books too are released commonly, and such functions are quite common. It is true, but the boarding house that was inaugurated in Chinchwad was not a common one, and the person whose biography was released was also not a common man. He was an extraordinary man who shunned limelight. Unknown has been his exceptional greatness. The boarding house in Chinchwad was built for the students of Manipur. Note the distance between Pune city of Maharashtra and districts Ukhrul and Vishnupur of Manipur, but Manipur has been connected with Maharashtra. Not only Manipur, the whole North East. Not many know that 109 students from North Eastern Bharat are studying in Maharashtra. Fifteen out of them belong to Manipur.

The Chinchwad boarding house is meant for these fifteen students. The inauguration function of that boarding house was marked with the release of the biography of the man who did the job of making connection between Manipur and Maharashtra. Was not that appropriate and congruous? There is no dearth of incongruities like such occasions. There was a cycle repair shop in Wardha (Maharashtra). A sign board on the shop read, "Poetry book written by an eminent poet is available here." Poor Panini, the grammarian, is criticized for having *Shva* (dog), *Yuva* (youth) and *Maghva* (Indra) tied in the same *sutra* (formula). There was no such incongruity in Chinchwad.

Who was that man? We know him as Bhaiya ji Kane. He is no more now. His full name is Shankar Diwakar Kane. Shankar is his name. Diwakar is his father's name and Kane is his surname, as mine is Vaidya. He was born in Nasik in 1924 and educated in Satara and Pune up to intermediate, then he served the Air Force, which he resigned after two years, and started education again. Graduated in 1946, joined the Satyagrah Movement to remove ban imposed on R.S.S. in 1948. Experienced prison life for six months, became R.S.S. *pracharak* after the ban was lifted. Remained *pracharak* for eight years in Karnataka, and then took retirement and accepted the job of a teacher for thirteen years, including the two years he served as teacher in a school run by Vanvasi Kalyan Ashram at Jashpur Nagar, district Raigarh in Chhattisgarh. He had developed affinity with the *Vanavasi* brethren. In 1972, he was attracted to North Eastern Bharat, and he directed the course of his mission toward Manipur, where he lived for a year in village Chingaloraya of district Ukhrool. Thereafter, he went to village New Tusoom, which adjoins Myanmar (Brahma Desh). It is the last village of India in that direction, which is terrorist infested, but Bhaiya ji liked this very same village. New language, new people, unknown environment, but robust courage. He settled there, learned the local language and started working among students of the place. Bhaiya ji was then 50, and the students were adolescents. They became friends with Bhaiya ji. Hardly had he lived in New Tusoom for a year and a half when he got the news of his mother's death, and so he left Manipur and returned to Maharashtra, and took job as a school teacher in Sangli in southern Maharashtra. He did not forget the North East. Every year he went to Manipur and brought students from there for educating them in Maharashtra. Most of the students belonged to Christian families, but they had such deep trust and belief in Bhaiya ji that they sent their children with him for studies to such a faraway place. During the period of two decades, from 1973 to 1993, he brought hundreds of students to Maharashtra, and made arrangements for their studies. When they went back to their original states, they carried with them the *Sanskars* of patriotism and one common nationality. The last three years of his life, from 1993 to 1996, he devoted to the *Vanvasi* region of district Thane. Vikramgarh, Jahwar and Wade were the centers of his social activities. To avoid dependency on others, he imparted tuitions, which were the source of his livelihood, not for making money. While teaching as per the school curriculum, he also imparted the lessons in patriotism and nationalism. Irrespective of the distance between the various places, he travelled just like one's movement from one room to another in a big house. He spared unlimited love for hundreds of families.

There is no dearth of people who have expertise in the politics of dissensions and disharmony in society. Bhaiya ji practiced the social ethics of connecting people and he connected innumerable people not only with himself, but with the nation and strengthened national integrity. That is why it was appropriate to release his biography with the inauguration of the boarding house, and that is why *Mananiya* Seshadri ji, a senior executive of R.S.S., attended the function at Chinchwad.

□

"The mountain raises its head and says, 'You too raise your height'. Ocean flourishes its waves and says, 'You too bring some depth to your psyche'. Do you understand what the fluctuating wave says? It says, 'Fill up your mind with sweet zeal'. The Earth says, 'Do not give up, even if your head is loaded with infinite loads'. The sky says, 'Overspread adequate enough to cover the whole world."

—Sohanlal Dwivedi

4

GIRISH PRABHUNE

'Samajik Samrasta Manch' is the name of an institution in Maharashtra. It was founded by the people connected with the R.S.S. In the year 1990, the institute sponsored an organization named '*Ghumantu Aur Vimukt Jati Vikas Samiti*', meaning a committee for the development of nomadic and free tribes. Aim of the committee has been the progress of the tribes stamped as criminals. Shri Bhikuji Idate, the *Karyavah* of the Maharashtra *Prant* of R.S.S., who himself belongs to the nomadic tribe, is president of the committee, and Girish Prabhune is the secretary. *Swayamsevaks* of Medha tehsil of district Solapur in southern Maharashtra narrated an event after the closing ceremony of a *Sangh Shiksha Varg* (R.S.S. training camp) in Solapur in May 1991. It was about a tribe called Phase Pardhi. British Government had stamped it as a criminal tribe. Attitude of the police about the tribe has not changed even after more than 50 years of Independence. Police arrested two young men of Phase Pardhi tribe. They never returned. The police told the people who enquired about the whereabouts of the two arrested young men that the two had committed dacoity on Minar Express, so police shot them dead. The questions as to how could the young men go from police custody to commit train dacoity has not been answered yet.

Girish Prabhune became restless on hearing the narrative of the events. He went to the localities of Phase Pardhi along with the R.S.S. workers, and roamed there for about a month, clueless, but he developed concern and love for to the tribe. He earned their confidence and became privy with many horrifying narratives. His heart melted for them. Here are some hair-raising narratives:

- A young girl named Baby Shahivya Pawar was raped in police custody. Subsequently, she was released. Her mother-in-law expelled her from the family because she had been raped.
- Jayashri Kasturya Bhonsle, after her marriage, went to live with her husband in Kidgaon. Two sons of police-supported Patel tied her husband Kasturya with a pole and raped Jayashri in his presence. The couple left the village after the incident, and complained the crime to police. No action was taken against the culprits even after a lapse of 7-8 years.
- Vashya and Javadya were brothers. Their mother remarried after their father's death. Police arrested the two brothers. When their mother went to the police station to inquire about her sons, she was told that both of them died, hence police buried their dead bodies without post mortem.

Hearing all those incidents, Girish Prabhune decided to work for the welfare of that unfortunate tribe. He selected a locality named Yamgarvadi of Tuljapur tehsil in district Solapur. A philanthropist, named Ramesh Chatuphale of Yamgarvadi, donated his 16-acre land to Prabhune's '*Ghumantu Aur Vimukt Jati Vikas Samiti*.' Now there are two boarding houses, built on that land, for 200 boys and girls. The children who earned their livelihood by roaming and begging in nearby villages are now studying and living in the said two boarding houses, which are named as 'Eklavya' and 'Shabri Mata'. After completion of project of the boarding houses in Yamgarvadi, another project of houses for the nomads has come up in village Magarsangvi. It is known as 'Rehabilitation Project'. Virtually, it is not rehabilitation, but the first dwelling project, because there was no regular and permanent dwelling for them before that. Now efforts are made to end their nomadism. Shri Girish Prabhune got himself well acquainted with most of their customs related to quarrels, ignorance, and poverty, which besieged them generation-after-generation, and with their tribal judicial system that was often un-just. They built trust in Girish Prabhune. His words attained respectability. Though nobody from outside the tribe gets even entry into their *panchayat* (village assembly), Shri Girish Prabhune is invited with honor. All that did not happen in a day. There were tough occasions when Prabhune had to undergo many touchstone tests. Here is an instance. It was decided to run a bakery in village Magarsangvi in order to provide job opportunities to villagers. Prabhune insisted that the bakery be inaugurated by a couple. This proposal dumbed all the Phase Pardhi community. No body spoke, neither yes nor no. All of them started gazing on each other's face. After sometime a man stood up and spoke, "*Uncle, please do not propose so. We do not include women in any auspicious ceremony.*" "Why?" asked Prabhune. "*What to tell you uncle, who can vouch for the chastity of any woman here? Uncle, please do not spoil our faith, and tell us something else. If you order we shall take even poison, but we shall not accept this proposal, which will spoil our faith.*" Girish Prabhune took a stand on his proposal. After a pause, another man stood and said, "*All these women are sinners. Their sin has to be owned by someone. All members of panchayat will have to pay penalty for that. Minimum number of the members in any of our functions has to be twenty-five. Is there anyone who is prepared to own the sin? Is there any one prepared to pay the penalty? Will you own the sin?"* Girish Prabhune explained the story further, "*It was an unexpected question. I was stunned for a while. Then I thought, 'Whether it is a question of sin or virtue, what should matter is the ultimate result." So I gathered all my courage and retorted, "Yes, I will own. What shall I have to do for that?"* The man replied, "*You will have to pay the penalty of rupees five thousand out of your income."* Within a moment I said, "*Though it is difficult, yet I will pay'. All of them started gazing at me. They did not expect this reply from me, but now they could not backtrack, nor could I. I paid the penalty through the hands of Mananiya Seshadri ji, the then Sah Sarkaryavah of the R.S.S., to their leader Shri Shivaji Rao, and what did Shri Shivaji Rao do with that money? He surprised everybody by donating that entire money for construction of a temple."*

Can anybody evaluate that incident? Can the incident be woven up in any interpretation of economics? Can any science of logic or rationality explain this? The degree of the great oblation for social change like this, occurring without any pomp and show, can be appreciated only if one is willing to look at it with unjaundiced view sans malice.

□

> *'A lady remembers her beloved who gave her a nose ring, but she forgets the beloved who gave her the nose.'*
>
> —**Adage**

5

THAKRE MAHARAJ

I happened to meet Thakre Maharaj in an annual fair of my village Taroda, district Wardha. (The translator of this book too had the opportunity to visit the said fair in village Taroda. He has given a brief account of the occasion, which is appended below, after this article, under the caption: 'Awesome flow of goodwill in village Taroda district Wardha in Maharashtra'). Normally, Thakre Mahararaj joins the fair every year and performs *kirtan* (congregational singing in praise of God) on *Ekadashi.* Meaning of *kirtan* in Maharashtra is different from that in vogue in northern India. In Maharashtra, it implies religious discourse, sermon, music and the art of theatrics. Traditionally, in Maharashtra two types of *kirtan* are in vogue, *Naradiya*, and *Varkari.* Thakre Maharaj belongs to *Varkari* sect. I had heard about him as he used to come to the village fair every year to perform the *kirtan*, without accepting any kind of *dakshina* (religious offering), or fees, unlike other *kirtan* performers, who bargain the amount of the *dakshina* before performance. He is an exception. He accepts only the travelling charges. Normally, he performs only for a day, so earlier I had not paid much attention on his unique trait. This year (2002) his *kirtan* continued for a week, along with the *ekadasi kirtan*, and sermons on

Adhyatm-Ramayan. It was the week devoted to *Ram Katha*, which concluded on 12th of February. I reached Taroda, district Wardha in Maharashtra the same day. That day the organizers of the fair wanted to offer some hospitality to him. Since they knew that Thakre Maharaj would not accept any money, they decided to honor him with some clothes, etc. He denied the offerings, but, due to the earnest insistence of the organizers, he touched the offerings, and then and there, distributed them to the assembled people. As per the Maharashtrian tradition two betel leaves, one coconut, and at least one rupee is given along with other offerings. Thakre Maharaj distributed even those small offerings. It was pleasure to know all that about him, so I wanted to meet this dedicated great man. I invited him to my residence, and he came. We had enough discussions, and I came to know that Thakre Maharaj was not a *sanyasi*. He was a householder. He belonged to village Ralegaon of district Yawatmal of Vidarbha. He owned a travel agency, and that was the means of his livelihood. He indulged in *dharmic* activities like *kirtan* and sermons, but he stuck to his decision that he would not charge anything for that. I guess that the glorified reputation of his desireless activities had spread to far-flung areas without any pomp and show, at least up to the sacred place known as Mahur in Marathwada. Mahur is about 250 km from our village, and the whole region is considered sacred by the followers of *Datta* and *Shakti* faiths. The famous Dattatreya temple is also built along with the temple of Bhagvati Devi in the Mahur fort. Traditionally, a *kirtan* performer is appointed in this temple for the whole life. The process of appointment is quite fantastic. Slips showing names of popular *kirtan* performers are piled at a place and only one of them is picked at random. The person whose name is written on that slip is appointed as the *kirtankar,* or the *kirtan* performer. That lucky one and his family are looked after by the temple management. The old *kirtankar* had expired a couple of years back, so a new one had to be appointed. Names of about 270 *kirtankars* were proposed. Some *kirtankars* proposed their own names and did their best to get the appointment. Thakre Maharaj was not from that ambitious lot, but someone who knew him cast a slip with his name in the lot. Name of Thakre Maharaj appeared on the drawn lot. He was surprised when he came to know of that, but he accepted the appointment as a gift from Bhagwan Dattatreya. He lives in Mahur for a month and performs *kirtan* and *pravchan,* etc. During that period, he is looked after by the temple management. As per the tradition of the temple, expenses incurred on living of the *kirtankar* and his family, throughout life, have to be borne by the temple. Thakre Maharaj defied this tradition. This year (2002), he lived in Taroda district Wardha in Maharashtra for a week, but he had brought with him eatables, raw, uncooked food stuff, and even a stove to cook his food himself.

We hear about such instances that took place in the ages of the *Purans.* I am reminded of the story of Kautsa, a disciple of sage Vartantu. He had attained fourteen branches of knowledge from his guru. After completion of his education, he asked his guru about the guru *dakshina* he should pay him. Vartantu told him that there was no need of any guru *dakshina* as he was contented with his (Kautsa's) services. Kautsa was not satisfied with his reply, and so he kept on insisting his request. That infuriated the sage, and out of anger he asked his disciple, "You have learned fourteen disciplines, so go and bring me fourteen thousand gold coins as guru dakshina." Now Kautsa was taken aback. From where would he bring that huge amount of money? He remembered Raghu, the emperor, who had conquered the world. He went to him, but it was like *Shivaratri* going to *Ekadashi* (both are the occasions for fasting). The emperor was a pauper, as he had donated all the wealth acquired in his world-conquest. He possessed nothing. Even his guests were fed in earthen utensils. Even then Raghu welcomed Kautsa, and asked him to stay. It is said that Kuber, the deity of wealth, caused rains of gold coins in the treasury of Raghu that night. All that wealth had come for Kautsa. Raghu asked him, "*All this wealth has come because of you, and for you, so you take away all that.*" Kautsa replied, "*I need only fourteen thousand coins for guru dakshina to my guru. I will not take even a single extra coin.*" The discussion prolonged for a long time between the two. The citizens of Ayodhya relished the unique discussion. Finally, Kautsa won.

It is a story of ancient times. Can such a thing happen in modern days of *Kaliyug*? Daily we see, hear, and read the news of unbridled greed, struggles for grabbing lakhs and crores of rupees. Often I ponder what would be the ultimate use of all the money one collects? Can one eat cash, gold or silver instead of food grains? Our culture teaches us, '*para dravyeshu loshtavat*', or, others' money is like clay clod. In our surroundings, we note competitions in snatching and grabbing.

Thakre Maharaj is a *grihasth* (house holder), not a *sanyasi*. He clads like a common man. I do not know his caste, but I regard him as a true *Brahman*. He masters and exudes all the qualities of a *Brahman*, which Bhagwan Buddha has narrated in the *Brahmanavagga* of the *Dhammapad*, and that is why he is adorable. Not only adorable, imitable also. It is such persons who make nation great.

* * *

'Awesome flow of goodwill in village Taroda, district Wardha in Maharashtra', as given by the translator. (Courtesy – his article on the village fair of Taroda district Wardha in Maharashtra, published by the Hindi daily *Punjab Kesari,* Delhi, on 20 March 2002, under title: '*Sadbhava ki dhara kya desh bhar me nahin bahai ja sakti'?)*

"I was lucky to participate in the unique fair in village Taroda district Wardha in Maharashtra, with my wife, for the last three days of the fete, and enjoy the hospitality of Shri Vaidya ji and his family. I was wonderstruck to find that relative prosperity and social homogeneity and harmony were living together in the village, something very rare in villages. For the last more than a hundred years, Magh Shukl Pratipada (South Indian Hindu calendar) is observed as the closing day of the eight-day annual fete at the tomb of Sant Kejaji Maharaj, a saint of Mali community (a backward class) of the village. The occasion earned wide and effective publicity since the year 1971-72 due to relentless efforts of a village social worker, late Shri Shridhar Govind Vaidya, who was one of the younger brothers of Shri M.G. Vaidya. Kirtan is performed every evening at the fete, by all Kirtankars, irrespective of their caste or creed. Professionally a butcher Shri Shekh Gulzar, a Muslim, was a reputed Kirtankar. It was he who convinced the butchers, all Muslims, to close their business on Hindu festivals and fetes. Nobody asks the caste or creed of the Vina holder, the chief Kirtankar, whose feet are touched with the foreheads of visitors of any creed or community. The Vina changes hands frequently to let other Kirtankars lead the Kirtan team and be entitled to get his feet touched by forehead of the Vina giver, and visitors.

The most wonderful feature of the fete was the traditional common kitchen, and the common dining on the closing day. The whole process of cooking, distributing food and dining was manned by the social service conscious team of volunteers from all castes and religions of the village without any check, controversy, objection or hesitation. There was no discrimination, at any stage, on the basis of caste, creed, social, academic or financial status of the persons involved in the social occasion that was truly aimed at bringing social homogeneity and harmony. Villagers subscribed funds to hold the vast common dining program. They established a big kitchen near the tomb and cooked rice, pulses, vegetables and chapatis jointly for more than ten thousand diners squatting with their own utensils on both sides of the village corridor, all barefooted, but none bareheaded. The prominent role of the Vaidya family and their admirers on each aspect of the fete was remarkable and quite visible despite their efforts to shun limelight, truly in accordance with the Sangh tradition. Village Taroda was once chosen a place by R.S.S. to hold its Karyakari Mandal Baithak. It appeared that the common dinner was arranged by a huge joint family. That is why Taroda is a unique village. Such a practice of common cooking and common dining is extremely rare in our villages even today.

The occasion enabled me to know that Shri M.G. Vaidya has been a good farmer also. We travelled on his bullock-cart to see his farms, well irrigated and lush green. He had a problem. One of his two bullocks, employed to plough his farms and shifting the agricultural products and goods, was taller than the other, so while under yoke the shorter one had to take extra load on his shoulder. The village fair had a bullock market also. Vaidya ji visited the market with the view to sell the shorter bullock and buy another one to match the height of the other. As an expert of bullocks, he inspected many bullocks, opened their mouths and counted their teeth to ascertain their age, etc. and had lengthy discussions on the efficacy of the bullocks with many farmers".

□

"As long as man is overpowered by the darkness of ignorance, he is the slave of Nature and must accept whatever comes as the fruit of his thoughts and deeds. When he strays into the path of unreality, the Sages declare that he destroys himself; because he who clings to the perishable body and regards it as his true Self must experience death many times."

—Paramananda, The Upanishads

6

BRAHMA DEV

Brahma Dev passed away on 24 February 2002. He was 82. Though it cannot be called an untimely death, it did cause agony. The witness to the agony was the hugeness of the condolence meeting convened to pay homage to Brahma Dev on 26 February 2002, and the deep feelings of oneness and affinity expressed in orations by the mourners. Who was Brahma Dev? A *pracharak* of the R.S.S. That was his identity everywhere. What does the word *pracharak* mean? Gradually, meaning of this word is being appreciated in public, though I cannot say that it has been understood by all. I say so, on the basis of experience I gained after I came to Delhi, and came into contact with media people. The literal meaning of the word *pracharak* may be a propagandist or a publicist, but the original meanings of all words are not always at par with their conventional meanings. The word *panigrahan* in Hindi means marriage, but with the word *pani* meaning hand and *grahan* meaning holding, every handholding cannot be adduced to mean marriage. The word *pracharak* has gained a new purport in, and because of, the R.S.S. *Pracharak* means a *Brahmachari*, a word that includes many attributes, such as celibacy and learning, etc. (perhaps, there are no single words in English language, which may be truly equivalent to words like *pracharak, Brahmachari*, *Dharma* or *Dhamma* and *Sanskar* – infers the translator). *Pracharak* means a person who performs the directed duties, and goes to any directed place. *Pracharak* means a sort of *Sanyasi*, though not wearing saffron attire, and not living uncommon life. Sant Jnaneshwar said, "Do not be uncommon with common people, "ALAUKIK NO HAVE LOKANPRATI." Dr. Hedgewar, the founder of the R.S.S., had determined to set the same goal for *pracharaks*. Brahma Dev looked like a common man, but he was uncommon. He had attained B.Sc. degree in the year 1942 with first position. In all examinations, he had scored first position only. He decided to become a *pracharak* of R.S.S.. His family opposed. His father was angry, and furiously ordered him, "*Get out, do not show me your face.*" Brahma Dev ji followed his order literally. He did not see his father for 19 years. That was the time like that only. The present president of the Akhil Bharatiya Marathi Sahitya Sammelan, Shri Rajendra Banhatti has written the story about his elder brother becoming a *pracharak*. His elder brother's name was Madhav Banhatti. He was beaten with the leather belt of R.S.S., when he joined R.S.S. Even then he became a *pracharak* in the year 1943.

Brahma Dev ji started his *pracharak* life from Ambala, and then he was transferred to Rajasthan. In due course, he became the *Prant pracharak* of Rajasthan *Prant*, which he carried on for 18 years, and then took over as the *Kshetra pracharak* of *Uttar Kshetra*, which comprises of Rajasthan, Delhi, Haryana, Punjab, Jammu Kashmir and Himachal. Thereafter, he was deputed to Vishwa Hindu Parishad, where he served as a member of the Kendriya Marg Darshak Mandal for many years.

Some of the mourners narrated their memoirs about Brahma Dev ji in the condolence meeting of 26 February. Shri Satyanarayan ji Bansal, the *Sanghchalak* of Delhi *Prant*, said, "Once upon a time Shri Guru ji, the second Sarsanghchalak, had gone to see Brahma Dev ji's mother. She asked Shri Guruji, 'You had taken Brahma Deva for one year, when that one year will be completed?' Shri Guru ji replied, 'What can I do? You named him Brahma Dev, and the days and years of Brahma Dev are not like those of mankind.' Shri Sohan Singh ji had become *pracharak* with Brahma Dev ji. He said, "Once I got some money, and spent a part of that without noting it down. When Brahma Dev ji came to know about it he asked me, 'Had you noted down the amount of money you received?' I said, 'No, I did not.' He asked me another question, 'Did you note down the amount you spent?' I replied, 'No'. Then he asked me, 'Can you spare some time?' On my saying yes he himself picked up a pen and paper and asked me, 'Tell me the amount of money you received and the details of the expenses.' I told him all that, and he jotted down. Finally, he instructed me, 'It is public money. Every paisa must be accounted for.' That was his methodology to train his colleagues."

Shri Bhairon Singh Shekhawat, the former Chief Minister of Rajasthan, and the present *Mahamahim* Vice-President of India, said, "Whenever there was a telephonic call from Brahma Dev ji telling me that he was coming to meet me I was scared even after becoming Chief Minister, for, I thought I might have committed some mistake. Whenever he called me to Sangh Karyalaya I went there without any worry."

I met Brahma Dev ji quite late, when he was an adult. Though, apparently, he looked very strict, yet in reality he was not so. He attracted people due to his affectionate behavior, which reminded me of a damp coconut having hard external cover, but full of sweetness inside.

□

> *"Everybody is a genius. But if you judge a fish by its ability to climb a tree, it will live whole life believing that it is stupid."*
>
> **—Albert Einstein**

7

'NYISHI' TRIBE

A new awakening is dawning in North-East Bharat. There are many tribes in that region, and Christian missionaries have converted some of them. Anti-national and seditious rebellions erupted due to the conversions, which in effect meant change of nationality. Nagaland, Mizoram, and Tripura, have been affected by the antinational activities, terrorism and rebellion in different degrees. The rebellion, aided, and abetted by Christians started in Nagaland. It continued for many years, and did not stop even after Nagaland became a separate state. Now there is a ceasefire agreement between the Naga rebels and Government of India, as if two nations were fighting against each other, and now they have agreed to ceasefire. The conditions of the ceasefire are strange. The rebels and the representatives of Government of India will not talk about the ceasefire in India. They will talk either in Thailand or in Europe. We have seen the rebellion of Mizo tribe also. They constituted the Mizo National Front. There is a political party with this name. It gives the impression that Mizo is a nation. The government abolished the rebellion forcibly, but gave Mizos a separate state named Mizoram. Today the population of this state is only seven lakh. It means that there may be thirteen Mizorams in Delhi metropolis. It was not even four lakh, when the state of Mizoram was carved.

How Mizos are running the state? They are banishing and driving *Chakma* Buddhists and the *Riyang* Hindus out of the state. When Rajiv Gandhi was the top Congress leader, the Congress manifesto had declared that the Mizo State Government would run in accordance with Christianity. That is the plight of secularism in our country.

The state of terrorism in Tripura is well known. NLFT (National Liberation Front of Tripura) is a banned organization. The name of the organization itself is dangerous – Liberation Front. Liberation from whom? Is Tripura a nation or a state? It is a matter of delight to note the rays of awakening in the antinational atmosphere of darkness. The Khasi tribal people are forsaking Christianity and returning to their own tribal faith. That is why the Christian missionaries are losing self-control in anger. They have forsaken the path of peace and raised a terrorist organization called Red Army. Years back this outfit had abducted a young man who was devoted in saving the Khasis from Christianity. His whereabouts are not known yet. No response to this incident has been expressed in India or Indian Parliament. During the British days only the Christian missionaries were permitted to enter that area. That is why and how Meghalaya, Nagaland, and Mizoram became Christian-majority states. Only Arunachal is saved, but it could not escape the vulturine eyes of the Christian missionaries. About a decade back there was not even a single Christian in Arunachal. Now they are eight percent of the population. Though there is ban on conversion, and the entry of Christian missionaries in Arunachal is also banned, but conversion continues. How is it so? As part of their strategy the missionaries have opened well-equipped hospitals and schools on the Arunachal-Assam border, on the land of Assam. They bring children and the sick from Arunachal to Assam region for education and treatment, and taking undue advantage of their poverty and ignorance they are converted to Christianity, and subsequently, they become the medium and accessories for further conversions.

Now rays of awakening are visible even in Arunachal, where tribes are getting organized to protect the traits of their community. The awakening is evidenced by the congregation convened by Nyishi tribe. They have founded an organization named "Nyishi Indigenous Faith and Cultural Society (NIFCS)." A convention of this outfit was held in village Mahalangun, which was attended by five hundred representatives of Nyishi tribe. The main address to the convention was that of Lamio Tanga, the chairman of the Arunachal Legislative Assembly. Shri Tanga is a leader of Congress Party. In his address, he said, "There is a danger to our faith from the Christian missionaries. We have no risk from Hindus, because Hindus do not convert. As per our Constitution Sikhs, Jains and Buddhists are, inherently, Hindus, but Hindus do not impose their rituals on them. It is regrettable that now a days people of Arunachal are forsaking their traditional reverence and faith. It was only to safeguard our reverence and faith that we left Tibet and came to Arunachal Pradesh. Our priests are responsible for creating impiety in our youth, and we, the adults, too cannot escape our responsibility in that case. It is due to our misbehavior that unwanted inclinations are spreading in our youth. Now, what is needed is that the priests should observe simplicity and economy in our rituals. Animal slaughter is not a compulsory part of our faith. It is due to the slaughter of Mithuns (a sort of bull slaughtered traditionally on sacramental occasions like marriage, etc. in Nyishi society) that their number is diminishing. We should ban animal slaughter. Priests should come forward for that. It is their duty to see that our people are saved from being converted to other religion."

Shri Tedi Techi is the president of this organization. He also addressed the convention. He said, "It is our own people who are trampling our moral values. Attraction for other religion is increasing. People of other religion are attacking our reverences. We must safeguard ourselves. The 1978-Act of religious freedom has failed in this respect." Three resolutions were passed in that convention. The first pertained to the demand that the conspiracy to change names of persons of Nyishi community while giving them certificates of their belonging to Scheduled Tribe must be stopped. In the second resolution, it was demanded that action must be taken against the government officials who, directly or indirectly, compel Nyishis to accept alien religion (Christianity). The third resolution demanded appointment of an independent officer for safeguarding the faith and reverences of the Nyishi tribe.

Indeed, laudable is the awakening of the self-consciousness in Nyishi tribe. It is that feeling which can integrate them with the national mainstream.

□

"The little space within the heart is as great as the vast universe. The heavens and the Earth are there, and the Sun and the Moon and the stars, fire and lightning and winds are there, and all that now is and all that is not."

—**Swami Prabhavananda,** *The Upanishads: Breath from the Eternal*

8

NEW *VANAPRASTH* ASHRAM

For Hindus, service is social work, not a religious work. We have thousands of religious institutions as well as religious establishments, but any service project will hardly be found annexed with them. On the contrary, service projects such as orphanages, lepers' homes and hospitals, etc. are always, compulsorily, annexed with Christian missionaries. No doubt, they may be using the service projects for propagation of their religion, but it cannot be denied that they do service works and treat them as a part of their religious activities. In reality, the concept of "*NAR SEWA: NARAYAN SEWA*", i.e. "*Service to Mankind is Service to God*" has been recognized in Hindu society also. That service works should be part of religion will be perceived if we look into the real meanings of certain words that are settled in the language of the words. No worship or liturgy is done in a Dharmashala, a guest house, then why should it be called a Dharmashala? A Dharmarth Aspatal has nothing to do with religious rituals, still it is called Dharmarth Aspatal. It is so because service, free service, has been accepted as part of religion. We have forgotten that tradition, so our religious establishments did not pay attention towards the developmental aspects of service.

A symposium was convened in Delhi in April 2001 because of the initiative of an organisation called Sewa International. Four learned people from Germany also participated in the symposium. They were Dr. Weber, Dr. Vilhem Dahar, Dr. Exal, and Dr. Swain. The subject for deliberation in the symposium was, "The Hindu Concept of Service and Western viewpoint." Dr. Weber said in his address, "In America it is a common perception that only Christian missionaries do service works. In Hinduism, there is no importance for service works, nay, they do not exist in Hinduism. Hindus believe that poverty and sufferings are caused by the sins committed during previous births and one has to suffer the result of those sins. Social disparity in India would have been eliminated if Hindus had accepted the diligence doctrine of Christian missionaries. In pursuance of this doctrine the poor would have worked harder, and the rich would have given money. Of late Hindus also started doing service works, but they got inspiration for that from Catholic Church, not Hinduism."

Shri Surya Narayana Rao, the former All India Chief of Service Projects of R.S.S., also addressed the symposium. He said, *"Service (Sewa) is the very foundation stone of Hinduism. Sant Tulsidas has said,* 'Par hit saris Dharma nahin bhai, Par pira sam nahin adhamai.' (There is no religion at par with benevolence. There is no ignobility at par with causing pain to others.)" The well-known *Sant* of Gujarat, Narsi Mehta's hymn preaches, "*Vaishnava jan to tene kahie je peer parai jane re.*" It means that the true believers in God (Vishnu) are only they, who feel pain of others. Therefore, it would be confusing to say that service works are not important in Hinduism. It is a well-known fact that there was a special impetus given by R.S.S. to Service Projects after celebrations of the birth centenary of R.S.S. founder Dr. Hedgewar, were over. Shri Dharm Vir Kohli, chief of the Delhi unit of Sewa Bharti, told the audience about the service projects of R.S.S. running in Delhi. He said that the service outfits were doing service works in 410 backward localities of Delhi. 110

whole timer *Vanaprasthis* (retired persons), 240 part-time workers, and 110 lady workers were engaged in the service projects. There were 1430 service projects running in Delhi, which comprised of *balvadis, Bala Sanskar Kendras*, tailoring classes, health service units, and technical training outfits. Ladies of well-to-do families have been making social bonds with ladies of the slum areas through programmes like *Kanya Pujan, Havan-Yajna,* and campaigns for freedom from intoxicants. Such programmes have strengthened the feelings of social harmony. Shri Shyamaji Gupta informed audience about the service outfits run by the *Vanvasi Kalyan Ashram.* He said, "The Kalyan Ashram runs twelve thousand service projects among forest dwellers, including 6200 schools. More than two lakh male and female students are getting education in these schools. We believe that poverty in our country has been caused due to the plunders by imperialistic Christian nations and not due to sins in previous births." The four erudite Germans were highly impressed after hearing the speakers in the symposium and reading literature published by Sewa Bharti. They assured to publish in newspapers of their country about the new Service awakening in Hindus.

It will be appropriate to mention here that the R.S.S.-inspired organisations such as Vishwa Hindu Parishad, Vanvasi Kalyan Ashram, Bharat Vikas Parishad, Vidya Bharti, Deen Dayal Shodh Sansthan, Akhil Bharatiya Vidyarthi Parishad, and Rashtra Sevika Samiti are engaged in social service works. Vishwa Hindu Parishad runs 50 service projects, Vanvasi Kalyan Ashram 33, Bharat Vikas Parishad 24, Vidya Bharti 58, and Rashtra Sewika Samiti runs 25 different service outfits with their own names. Apart from these, 570 Service Projects are conducted by the Sewa Bharti. Total number of the service projects run by all these organisations is about 35000, which comprise about 4000 health care centres, more than 17 thousand academic outfits, and more than 13 thousand other service units. Why such detailed particulars of the service projects? Because there runs a silent revolution of social service in our society without publicity. That is changing the mentality of society. We too must contribute in that. After completion of 60 years of age, when we are free from family obligations, we should present ourselves to be engaged with social activities. This should be taken as modern *Vanaprastha Ashram*, and we should be ready right now to utilize the remaining life obligingly. Such dedicated engagements will expedite the required social change.

□

> *"Rare are the persons whose mind, speech and body are filled up with the nectarian spiritual reward of merit, who delight the three worlds by their manifold beneficences, and who delight by magnifying even a molecule of others' merits to the extent of a huge mountain."*
>
> **—Adage**

9

MARAADA: ATTACK AND COUNTER ATTACK

There are so many oddities, which are not available anywhere in India except Kerala. There is no political party known as Muslim League anywhere in India, but it is there in Kerala. It was Muslim League that caused truncation of Bharat; got Pakistan, but even there the party hardly exists. There is no Muslim League in Bangladesh, the former East Pakistan, where even this name does not exist. In Pakistan, the former West Pakistan, only name of the party exists, but in Kerala, a state in Bharat, Muslim League is the name of a powerful party. Parliamentarian Banatwala, a resident of Mumbai, is one of the top leaders of the party in Kerala. He does not contest elections from Mumbai, he contests from Kerala, where he wins and comes to Lok Sabha. It is ironical that both, Congress and Communists, said to be secular parties, recognize Muslim League as a secular party. The Muslim League of Kerala has two groups: one is usually in alliance with Congress, and the other with Communists. Disgraced because of its role in truncation of Bharat, the Muslim League was given prestige by Congress. 'Messiah of secularism', Pandit Jawaharlal Nehru declared publicly that Muslim League of Kerala was different from the Muslim League of northern India. It was necessary for the Congress Party to support Muslim

League for the success of its strategy to pull down the first Communist government of Kerala. So Congress kept in abeyance all its secular principles and certified Muslim League as a secular party. It forged an alliance with Muslim League. Congress pulled down the Communist government and gave Muslim League respectability by ascending it on the prestigious throne of power in Kerala. Although Congress had branded Muslim League as a secular party, yet Muslim League did not leave its communal politics. As soon as it came to power with Congress, it carved out a new district called Mallapuram, which comprised of Muslim majority population. Those acquainted with the state of affairs there opine that the new district resembled a small Muslim state, like a mini Pakistan.

As soon as the symbol of slavery and communal goondaism was demolished in Ayodhya (Uttar Pradesh) on 6 December 1992, the fundamentalist Muslims, whose number and influence supersedes the rest, lost their self-control everywhere in the country. In Kerala also they behaved likewise. Although the faddish designs of fundamentalists faded away elsewhere after 1992, at some places they had to face agonizing consequences, yet in Kerala each 6th of December is marked with craze of the fundamentalist Muslims. General strike is observed in entire Kerala on that date, and how can a Muslim-sponsored strike go peacefully? That continued year after year, but after December 2001 there have been some visible changes.

As usual, on 6 December 2001 a violent strike started. Target of the attack were Hindu devotees of Shabari Malaya pilgrimage. Muslims attacked the main gate of the Shabari Malaya temple situated on the Pathanaamatittha hill. They damaged and plundered the shops of Hindus, and burned the district office of B.J.P. They snatched the holy bags containing coconut, etc. from the devotees proceeding on stairs of the temple and broke the heads of the devotees with the coconuts. Though such incidents were customary, this time, the 6 December 2001, the devotees decided to retaliate and teach a lesson to the attackers. All the Hindus forgot their political differences and got together. They called for a whole Kerala *bund* (close the whole Kerala) on 10 December 2001 to express opposition to the violent activities of 6 December. It got overwhelming support from whole Kerala, which thwarted the strike of 6 December. Unlike 6 December there was no violence on 10 December. The hot rumours such as "Mosques burned", "Muslims burned alive", etc. brought no result; on the other hand, credibility of the fundamentalist Muslims suffered a heavy damage.

Fundamentalist Muslims can never live peacefully. They chose a coastal village called Maraad in district Kozikod (Calicut) for their misadventure. Most of the menfolk were out for pilgrimage to Shabari Malaya and most of the population left behind in the village comprised of women and children. With the intention to take advantage of such a situation, there started proclamations on loud speakers installed on roof tops of mosques. Rioters assembled with bottles filled with petrol. Houses and concerns of Hindus started burning. Two Hindus were murdered. Seeing the scenario, the village womenfolk came on road fearlessly, and with kitchenware in their hands they retaliated. Nearby villagers came to help the retaliating womenfolk. The invaders had to flee. Three of them were killed.

Subsequently, governmental activities started. Congress, led coalition leader Shri K. Muralidharan, and district collector, rushed up to Maraad. They planned to visit the houses of the defeated invader Muslims. Getting clue of the plan, the ladies came out of their houses and *gheraoed* the government team. They insisted that the team must first see the houses of the affected Hindus, because Muslims had attacked them first, and assess the extents of their loss. The ferocious posture of the women compelled the government team to inspect the damaged houses of the Hindus first.

A remarkable result of the attack by fundamental Muslims was unity among the Hindu fishermen. Fishermen in Kerala are called 'Araya'. Their 42 institutions (Araya Samajam), got together on a common platform. A community outfit named 'Jan-Sabha' was founded. Poojya Swami Chidanand Puri Maharaj attended the first meeting of the Sabha. Shri Gopala Krishnan, the *Sah Prant pracharak* of Kerala branch of R.S.S., also addressed the meeting. The aim of the fundamentalist Muslims is to drive out the Hindu fishermen from the coastal area of Malabar. Earlier they had succeeded in shunting away the Hindu fishermen, with the same technique of invasions, from the coastal areas near district Mallapuram, but the new awakening among the Hindus has stopped ill-intentions of the fundamentalist Muslims. It was the miracle that happened because of the awakening in society.

□

"Do you believe in miracles? Well, you should. In fact, life itself is a big miracle. There are so many things that are beyond our understanding. There are two ways to live. You can live as if nothing is a miracle, you can live as if everything is miracle."

—Stephen Hawking

10

VASANT RAO TARE

Buldhana is the name of a district in Vidarbha region of Maharashtra State. Nandura is the name of a Tehsil in that district. There was a grand programme in Nandura on 25 January 2002 to bid farewell to a 87-year-old local doctor named Vasant Rao Tare, and I attended the programme as chief guest. The send off marked Dr. Tare's leaving the city forever to go to his son Dr. Arun Tare. Dr. Vasant Rao had devoted 60 years of his life in medical profession in Nandura city. The word 'profession' is not adequate enough to honor the way Dr. Tare rendered medical services to public, because he never viewed his work as a profession. That does not mean that he did not charge the patients. He charged them because he had to run his household, but, along with the fees he earned peoples' love, trust and honor also. Love, trust and honor cannot be demanded. Dr. Tare also never demanded, but all that came to him automatically and silently, without any commotion of publicity. He never worked for money. He did the work of the Rashtriya Swayamsevak Sangh. He worked as *Nagar Karyavah*, *Ghosh Pramukh*, and handled many responsibilities such as *Jila Karyavah* to *Jila Sanghchalak*. He became a *Swayamsevak* in Ahmadnagar, where he had gone to attain medical education. Inspired by Dr. Hedgewar, a *Swayamsewak*, named Babu Rao More, had gone from Chandrapur to Ahmadnagar for getting medical education. Shri Tare got introduced to Shri More and became a *Swayamsewak*. Dr. Tare should be regarded as a very lucky *Swayamsewak*, because he was one of the batch of the 25-30 trainees sworn into R.S.S. by Dr. Hedgewar himself in the year 1936. Dr. Vasant Rao recalls, "Since that day there was a drastic change in my nature, and my life as a Sangh Sanskarit man started since that time."

In the year 1939, Dr. Tare came to Nandura and started his medical practice there. In 1965, the then R.S.S. *pracharak* of district Buldhana, Shri Vasant Rao Kasabekar gave an idea to Dr. Tare that an urban cooperative bank should be founded in Nandura, and Dr. Tare should take initiative for that. Dr. Tare replied, "There are many banks in Nandura, why a new bank"? Kasabekar ji replied, "Other banks do only business. We should have a bank, which should do the business skilfully, but some social work should also be done by it. Its working should reflect that the bank officials do not watch their self-interest, but the interest of the society."

Dr. Vasant Rao Tare accepted his proposal, and 'Nandura Urban Cooperative Bank' was founded in the city. For about 20-25 years Dr. Tare was an officer with the bank. In a programme convened in Bidaagee, he said, "Vasant Rao Kasabekar had asked me that the bank officials should not watch their own interest. I followed his words literally. The instance of Aarya Chaanakya has guided me. For his private work Aarya Chaanakya never used light of the lamp lit with the oil afforded by government. Another lamp with oil fetched from his house was lit for doing his private work. I never took loan from the bank, nor did I employ any of my relations in the bank."

How many bank or government officials today really follow Dr. Tare's way of working? Now after giving 60 years of services to Nandura, when he made up his mind to leave the place, public decided to honour him. Dr. Tare expressed his unwillingness for the honour. He said, "What supernatural work have I done to deserve the honour? I am a common citizen, a common doctor, an ordinary man living family life. My experiments in authenticity in whatever I did in society brought me love and respect. What peculiarity does it have to beget me the honour?"

His reluctance to accept the honour got publicity, so the organisers of the occasion told him, "We want to honour you as a pretext to raise funds for the aid of the Vivekananda Vachanalaya of our city, and the Vanavaasee Aashrama in nearby Jamod. We know that you will not accept even a single paaee from the endowment." Then Dr. Tare accepted the proposal, but put a condition that the programme should not be called a "*Satkar Samaroh*" (function for a courteous welcome). *It should be called a send-off.*" It was in that send-off function on January 25, 2002 that I had gone there to participate. The collected endowment money was announced. Dr. Tare himself subscribed ₹ 9001/- to that, and the entire amount was given to the Vivekanand Vachanalaya, Nandura and the Vanvasi Ashram, Jamod.

We hear lots of discussions about principles and conducts. Principles remain on one side, and conducts, separately, on the other side. In most of the cases, principles remain mere unused figments of imagination and empty talks. Only conduct upon them can bring glory and radiance. Dr. Tare's conduct belongs to that category. He happens to be an ordinary medical practitioner, an ordinary man of a tehsil, but country is made great by the conduct of majority of such common people. Having a couple of persons of Himalayan heights and the rest of society with heights of ant-hills can never be symptom of a healthy character of society. Will you call a man healthy, or sick, if he or she has got some organs of body sturdy and robust, while other parts are very feeble and frail?

□

> Yaksha to Yudhishthira, "*Who is toughest enemy to win? Which is never ending malady? Who is saint? Who is wicked "? Yudhishthira replied, "Anger is toughest enemy to win. Greed is never ending malady. One who desires weal for all beings is saint. One who is devoid of mercy is wicked.*"
>
> **—Adage**

11

'RUGNA MITRA' (FRIEND OF THE SICK)

I was lucky to have got an opportunity to be present as chief guest in a heart-touching programme in Mumbai on 20 April 2002. It was convened on behalf of the Nana Palkar Memorial Society to celebrate the *Amrita Mahotsav* of '*Rugna Mitra*' Dr. Madhav Rao Paralkar. '*Rugna Mitra*' (friend of the sick) was the title given to Dr. Paralkar, not by government, but by public. It did not fall on him like sudden rain drops, he had earned it by dint of his own virtuous deeds.

Who was this Nana Palkar in whose memory the said society was organised? Nana Palkar was a *pracharak* of R.S.S. He was not highly educated, but was highly talented. The biographies of Dr. Hedgewar and Shri Guru ji, written by Nana Palkar, are the ornaments of biographical literature in Marathi language. His treatise titled *Israel: Chhalakadun Balakade* (*Isral: From Tortures to Strength*) earned him world fame. Nana was a good poet also. Well known are also his collections of patriotic songs. He passed away in 1967 when he had hardly lived 49 years, but then he was the *Prant Karyavah* of Maharashtra branch of R.S.S. Before that he was the *Bauddhik Pràmukh* of the branch. His way of living inspired Dr. Madhav Paralkar, who was a medical graduate, but he did not practice his profession for his family, because he had no personal family. He too was a *Sangh pracharak*. The terminology of *Sangh pracharak* is gradually understood by people. A *Sangh pracharak* remains unmarried. He does not get any honorarium. There is no room for giving him any money, because he gives his whole time for only *Sangh Karya*. As far as respect is concerned, he does not expect it as he chooses the role of a foundation stone. Stones for foundation are never decorated. A *Sangh pracharak* is a sort of *Sanyasi*, an ascetic with a little difference. *Pracharaks* do not wear saffron robes. Is it a part of *Sangh* training? No. Sant Jnaneshwar Maharaj taught that. He has said, "*Alaukika Nohaave Lokaan Prati*." It means that while living with people, one should not look like an unworldly being, that is why Dr. Madhav Paralkar, though a qualified man, lived like a *pracharak*, and kept himself engaged in *Sangh Karya*. When in 1967 Nana Palkar passed away Dr. Paralkar thought that something should be done to perpetuate the memory of that great soul dedicated in the service of the nation. He met Shri Guru ji, the second *Sar Sanghchalak* and expressed his desire. Shri Guru ji supported his intention. Dr. Madhav Paralkar was a resident of Mumbai, a terrific metropolis, where everyone is ever busy. Everyone lives life of strict rules, as if part of an automatically regulated grand mechanism, indifferently, curtly and tersely. Dr. Madhav Paralkar decided to flow current of love and affection in that dry and mechanised life. In the year 1968, he founded the 'Nana Palkar Memorial Society'. He was alone. Later he got company of Dr. Ajit Phadake, the neurologist of world fame. Now Dr. Phadake is the president of the Memorial Society.

In Mumbai, there are certain unparalleled modern medical facilities, which are not available elsewhere. So many people bring their sick relatives to Mumbai for treatment. For cancer patients, it appears to be obligatory to go to Mumbai for treatment in the renowned Tata Cancer Hospital. The Society came forward to provide accommodation to the patients and their attendants coming from outside Mumbai. Since the Society had no building and the connected provisions, Madhav Paralkar started accommodating the patients in the houses of his friends and acquaintances. For a *Sangh pracharak*, it is natural to have very close and personal relations with many families. So Madhav Paralkar used his acquaintances to provide temporary shelter to the patients. In due course, *Sangh* arranged a small abode for them, though a bigger house was required. Shri Afzalpurkar, the Commissioner of Mumbai Municipal Corporation, appreciated the work of Dr. Paralkar and gave him a plot of land on lease. Then Madhav Paralkar set himself after the mission of constructing a building on that plot. He took contributions from not only the rich, even common people were motivated by him to contribute ₹ 5/- or ₹ 10/- for the building. The contributions were adequate to have the 'Rugna Sewa Sadan' in the seven-storeyed building that was built with all facilities. A patient and two of his/her attendants can stay there for a month. Hot water for bath, food on nominal rates, and transport facilities also on nominal rates are available for them. Lift facility exists in the building. Thus, the patients and their attendants get a new home, far away from their homes, on quite nominal rates. A brief account of the services and the financial aid given to the patients during financial year 2001-02 is given below: Total number of the resident patients – 1777. Out of them cancer patients – 1520, heart patients – 77, kidney patients – 51, brain patients – 29, others – 100. The Rugna Sewa Kendra has got a medicine bank, named 'Madhu Aushadhi Pedi'. This *Aushadhi pedhi* gave ₹ 6,56,377/- to the patients as financial help.

A branch of Nana Palkar Memorial Society is active in Borivali, a suburb of Mumbai. 2,344 patients got due service there in the year 2001-02. Credit for all those services goes to Dr. Madhav Paralkar. He completed 75 years of his life, so a ceremonial felicitation for him was organised in 2002 in Poddar college auditorium. The following article narrates what type of man Dr. Paralkar is, and what type of techniques does he adopt to establish affinity with people.

□

"Do you love your fellow men? Where should you go to seek for God – are not all the poor, the miserable, the weak, Gods? Why not worship them first? Why go to dig a well on the shores of the Ganga? Believe in the omnipotent power of love. Who cares for these tinsel puffs of name?"

—Swami Vivekananda

12

WHAT IS THAT SOIL, WHICH MAKES – RESOLUTELY ASSIDUOUS AND COURAGEOUS PEOPLE?

The *Amrita Mahotsav* function, to celebrate the 75th year of the life of Dr. Madhav Paralkar, the main figure of the 'Nana Paralkar Memorial Society' marked the publication of a classical work containing description of his meritorious attainments. It is a collection of the articles written in his glory. It contains many memoirs also. The following three memoirs from that work make one ponder over the question; '*What is that soil which makes such Karma-Veeras*', the resolutely assiduous and courageous people? The first is the one written by Dr. Ajit Phadake. Dr. Phadake writes:

Unbiased Service (*Nirapeksha Sewa*)

"On 20 June 1989, I underwent bypass surgery of my heart. I was admitted in Beach Candy Hospital. Unconscious by medicines, I had no idea about the place and time. On gaining consciousness, I opened my eyes I saw Madhav Paralkar standing nearby with the same smiling face. I was in the hospital for about two weeks. Madhav Paralkar visited me daily during morning and evening, without even a single miss. During that period he not only served me but also received the visitors who came to see me. Pressure on my mind was gone. Since then our mutual closeness increased to the extent that he became like a member of my family. "*I observed that Madhav served other people also with the same close affinity as he did to me. His steadfastness in service has been continuous for the last 35 year. In serving the sick, Madhav never discriminated between a Swayamsevak and an unknown person. His steadfast perseverance in service makes him almost a member of the families of the sick.*

'*In 1995 we needed ₹ 75 lakh to construct building for the Rugna Sewa Kendra.* Madhav girded up his loins for that mission. He had no experience of collecting funds. He discussed the issue with other members of Society and chalked out a plan. Daily at 7 a.m. he contacted me on phone and informed me whom to meet. Next day he would phone again to inquire about result of the meeting. It was because of his steadfastness that I could meet many well-to-do people and collect enough money. The construction work started, and on 13 April 1997 the 'Rugna Sewa Kendra' was inaugurated methodically. *Poojaneeya* Pandurang Shastri Athavale, the creator of the *Swadhyay Andolan*, was present on the occasion for offering his blessings. That was the happiest day of Madhav Paralkar's life."

The Magical Touch

Abhaya Mokashi is associated with film industry. The title of his write up in English is *Medicine Man with Magic, and Miracles without Medicine.*

Shri Mokashi narrates his own experiences:

"On 3 June 1992, our bus turned over near Indore. I suffered serious injuries. I was unconscious for some time. All the passengers except me got down, and two of them, somehow, removed me from the bus. I gained consciousness after a few hours, but I was illusioned about the place I belonged to. In due course, I came to

Mumbai, and went to our family doctor. He gave me some oils. CT scan revealed that I had suffered many injuries on brain. My spinal cord was injured. There was a sort of insensitivity in my waist. It was difficult even to walk. Though the oil therapy was beneficial, I had pain in whole body. Pain flowed up to my waist if someone touched even my hair. I started travelling from one to another department of the hospital. Doctors could not diagnose the source of pain. They thought it was my mental malady, so they advised to consult a psychotherapist they said that there could be no pain in hair.

"It was that time when my maternal uncle Rajat Kulkarni called me to *Sangh Karyalaya*, where I met Dr. Paralkar for the first time. The moment he saw me he asked, "Do you have some health problem?" He must have noted agony on my face. I narrated to him the whole episode, right from the accident.

"May I examine you?" Dr. Paralkar asked me. I accepted with a thought of letting one more doctor examine me. He asked me to remove my kurta and stand straight with my back facing window. He stood behind me and looked at my spinal cord for about 15 seconds, but did not touch any part of my body. "Now come here and lie upside down. I have understood your problem", he said. There was no sign of any injury on my back or waist; even then he touched the points where there was pain. I thought that the man must have been gifted with some divine sight. He did not see my X-ray report or CT scan. He believed in my statement that there was pain on touching my hair.

"He asked me to lie with my face up, and covered my body with a thin cloth. He then started giving vibrations to my soles. Sensitivity of the vibrations was limited up to ankles. I had no feeling of any vibration further. My friend and maternal uncle saw the vibration on the cloth that covered me. The doctor said that he would treat me, but it would take six to nine months, and would start the treatment if I agreed. Had I disagreed I would have been compelled for mental treatment, so I agreed. He asked me to report at 7.30 a.m. daily, and I followed, regularly, though the frequent jerks he gave me as part of the treatment were painful. He pressed and massaged at certain points. After a few days I heard sound coming from my body, head to heels, often painful for some moments. Though he had said that the treatment would take six to nine months, I felt miraculous developments. I felt vibrations from my soles to head.

"During the meetings, I asked Dr. Paralkar hundreds of questions, which he replied with pleasure. That time he was above 60, but very strong. Now he has completed 75, but he may surpass youth in strength even today. You spend a few moments with Dr. Paralkar, and you will feel a child's spirit is ingrained inside his great personality. You give him a chocolate and see a childlike pleasure on his face.

"He did not charge me even a single paisa for my treatment. On the other hand, he said that it was my positive attitude and trust in him that recovered me so soon."

Absence of Vanity

What would have been the lifestyle of persons like Dr. Madhav Paralkar, so dedicated in social service? Does vanity of service obsess them? It would not be unnatural even if it does obsess, but please do read the following memoir before arriving at any conclusion on the subject. The memoir is written by Nagpur-based Avinasha Sangavai, who is in-charge of the Hedgewar Rakta Pedhee (blood bank).

"It was 1980-81, I had to take my younger brother to Mumbai. Some defect had been noticed in a valve of his heart. He was to be admitted in K.E.M. Hospital. We were staying with an acquaintance. Dr. Paralkar came to see us there. He told my brother that there was nothing to worry, as the doctors of K.E.M. Hospital were known to him. "They will examine the case, but we must hurry up. Don't worry, I am with you", he said.

"We were three. Accommodation was a problem, which we told Dr. Paralkar. He asked us not to worry and go to *Sangh Karyalaya* at Dadar. We went there. I observed the daily routine of Dr. Paralkar. He went out daily early morning and returned any time during night. He moved around by scooter. I noted that one night he returned very late. He looked tired and enervated. I saw him going to kitchen and coming back within two minutes. I was curious to know whether the doctor had dinner, or not. I could not sleep due to uneasiness. I went to his room and saw him preparing for sleep. I asked him, "What about your food?" He replied, "I had made a mistake. I was so busy that I forgot to inform the Karyalaya in evening that I would be late and have dinner. I have drunk sufficient water, and now I am going to sleep."

"I was restless. I aroused the kitchen in-charge, and told him that the doctor was hungry, so he should be given food. He replied that he had no message about the doctor's dinner. I requested him to arrange some food for him. He replied that he could not do anything because the cook had gone home. I lost my balance, got angry, and told him, "He is working so hard for the patients, who will feed him? Does he have a private residence"? Discussion prolonged. He was not ready to move. The doctor heard my voice and came out of his room. He asked me, "Avinasha, why are you scolding him? It was my mistake." Doctor apologised to him and went back to his room. I also went to my room. I was feeling guilty. I thought that I also could cook. Why should I not cook some food? I went to kitchen, cooked *khichadi* (a dish of rice and pulse mixed together), curry, and roasted *papads* (a thin, crisp and salted bread). I called doctor for the meal. He came and started taking it, but his eyes were full of tears. I started brooding, "Is discipline for man, or man for discipline?" I saw that the fatigue was missing from his face after he took the meal, and we talked for about two hours. I felt like thanking the kitchen in-charge, but for him I could not get related so intimately with this great man. Before going to bed I went to the room of the kitchen in-charge, and aroused him. He said, "You are right, but what could I do? I do not know cooking. I was not asleep." He then started weeping loudly. I thought that my disposition achieved what my anger could not.

A close affinity has been established between Dr. Paralkar and me. I live in Vidarbha, doing the work of *Rakta Pedhee* (blood bank), but I am ever eager to meet Dr. Paralkar."

□

"There should be no doubt in deciding whether circumstances create a leader, or a leader creates circumstances. It is a leader who creates circumstances."

—A proverb

13

WORLD VEDA SESSION

Panjala is the name of a village in district Trishoora in Kerala State. It is situated on the banks of the holy river Bhuratpuja. All of a sudden it earned world fame because of the World Vedic Convention convened from 3 to 7 April 2002. It was named 'World Veda Satram', the World Veda Session. About 1000 representatives participated in the convention, one hundred from outside Kerala, and a few from foreign countries also. Interestingly, a Muslim representative named Kunju Ahmad also attended the convention. He performed *Namaaz* whenever it was the time for *Namaaz*, and the proceedings of the convention were silent on the *Namaaz* moments. When asked why, in spite of being a Muslim, had he come to attend the Vedic Convention, he replied, "I knew that God's Consciousness is present here." Whenever Kunju Ahmad expressed his desire to perform *Namaaz* during the convention, the organisers provided him a mat. Kunju Ahmad said with pleasure that nobody disturbed him when he performed *Namaaz*. Panjala is a small village, with only ten houses of Namboodri Brahmans. Out of those ten, there are three *Rig Vedics*, two *Yajur Vedics*, and five *Saama Vedics*. The *Vedic Pundits* who sing *Saama Veda* are not available everywhere. Panjala should be felicitated for preserving the tradition of *Saama Veda*.

The convention was inaugurated by Railway Minister for State Shri O. Rajagopala. He belongs to Kerala. It was presided over by *Acharya* Narendra Bhushana. The prominent among the subjects of the papers read and discussed in the convention were 'Democracy in Vedic Age', 'Status of Women in Vedic Age', 'The Art of Presentation of the Vedas,' and 'The Scientific Aspects of the Vedic Customs and Traditions'. Dr. Fatima Bibi, the Sanskrit scholar, also took part in discussions on the '*Status of Women in Vedic Age*'.

Michel Donino, a scholar from France, displayed a slide show on the topic "*Indus-Saraswati Civilization and its Relation with Vedic Age.*" While presenting the programme Donino said, "The Archaeological excavations in the regions of Sindhu and Saraswati have given ample evidences to establish the fact that the Vedic Culture flourished on the banks of Indus and Saraswati." The slide show proved that the Aryan Invasion theory propounded by Marxists and followers of Macaulay was totally baseless. Parvati, a young girl, aged 25, from Kannamukalan, earned profuse applause from the surprized representatives when she sang melodiously four *Sooktas* from the *Rig Veda*. She had learned the *Veda* in her early childhood from her grandfather. Parvati said, "Nobody has objected so far to my studying the Vedas. In fact all the Hindu organizations and institutions have encouraged me."

The *Vedas* are the mines of knowledge, and knowledge cannot be monopolised by any particular class. It is our old tradition. The course of education prescribed for the *Kshatriya* rulers included '*Trayee*', i.e. study of three *Vedas* also. *Trayee* included only three *Vedas*, viz. *Rig Veda, Saama Veda*, and *Yajur Veda*. Later other classes of society stopped studying the *Vedas* as it provided little scope of financial and other mundane gains. The *Vedic* study was confined only in Brahmana class, which had to study the *Vedas* because of the ordain, "Brahmanena nishkaarano Vedodhyeyah." It means that a Brahmana should study the Vedas without any reason.

Circumstances have changed today. Women and non-Brahmanas are also studying the *Vedas*. New *Vedic* centres have provisions for that. Shri M.K. Kunjal from Kerala, who is a leader of the backward class, and winner of the 'Ambedakar Award', while condemning the opinion of Marxists, said, "Marxists use the name of Vivekananda and Shri Narayana Guru for bad publicity. Why don't they themselves convene *Vedic* conventions or lectures on the *Vedas*? Dr. Joseph Kolayana, a scholar in Christianity, who taught English in many Indian and Western colleges, also participated in the convention. Now even the physicists of the West are acknowledging the importance of the *Vedas*.

The *Vedas* are our most valuable trust. We should thank the ritualist *Brahmanas*, who have been maintaining the tradition of learning the *Vedas* for thousands of years, as a result of which the *Veda Samhita* is available even today in its pure form. Now it is the need of the hour that the *Vedas*, which are the reservoir of knowledge, should be studied, and the whole world gets the knowledge.

□

> *"The Earth is His. To Him belong those vast and boundless skies. Both seas within Him rest, and yet in that small pool He lies."*
>
> **—Atharva Veda**

14

A PECULIAR '*SAHYADRI*'

I have seen the Himalaya 2-3 times, from the side of Kangra, Hamirpur, Dharamsala, Simla, Kullu, Manali, Dalhouzi, as well as from the side of Nainital, Naini Shikhar, Gangotri, Kedarnath and Badrinath also. *Mahakavi* Kalidas has eulogized it profusely. He has named it as *Nagadhiraj* (king of mountains) and *Devatatma* (spirit of divinity). He has described it as "Anant Ratna Prabhav" i.e. infinite source of gems. All these attributes belong to the Himalaya, but I have noticed its weakness also. It is very weak. It moves even with slight wind storm. A little rain can make it slide. I have seen mountain Sahyadri also, many times. Though it is not as high as the Himalaya, yet it is very strong. Be it windstorm or a hurricane, it would not move. Are the people living around Sahyadri also immovable like it in tempestuous circumstances? Yes, I am going to introduce a Sahyadri-type character.

That Sahyadri in human form expired on 29 March 2002. Then he was 87, so it cannot be termed as untimely death. I read the news of his death in Marathi daily *Tarun Bharat*. The news described that he died of old age. I wrote a letter to his wife, but while writing I paused for a while when I recalled the said published news. Old age and Babaji? My mind was not ready to synchronize the two words. Name of this *Sahyadri* was Babaji Date, full name was Shri Krishna Dattaatreya Date. *Shri Krishna* being his own name, Dattatreya his father's name, and Date, the name of his clan. But we knew him only as Babaji Date. He was born in Yavatmal, a district head quarter in Maharashtra, about 150 kilometres away from Nagpur. Yavatmal was his *karmabhoomi* and he passed away there only. P.G. Sahasrabuddhe was one of his friends. He writes, "Babaji Date symbolised grit, determination, and firm resolve. He symbolised courage to welcome change, not only to welcome, but to stand to fight. Babaji Date symbolised metaphysics, deification of Hindutva. Babaji Date symbolised simple living but high thinking. Babaji Date symbolised multiplicity of industries, incessant industriousness, constant toil. He symbolised the field in which a common person would be scared even to step, but he would intrude and earn glory."

Babaji Date was M.A. in English literature and Economics, and a Law graduate. He taught English in a government college in Nagpur. Later he became a Principal in Amalnera in Khandesh, a part of State of Maharashtra. As a worker of R.S.S., he was imprisoned after Gandhiji's assassination on 30 January 1948. His wife, Mangala Tai, was a part-time teacher in a school. She was removed from that job because she was wife of a *Sangh* worker. His friends, who had gone to jail to meet him advised him to resign so that he could get another job easily after the jail term. Babaji retorted, "My luck was scripted by God, not by the Board of Education of Khandesh."

Shri Ram Kapse, the Kalyan-based teacher, was BJP MLA, and MP. Now he is Lt. Governor of Andaman Nicobar. He was a teacher in a college started by Babaji Date, in its initial stage, at the Andaman Nicobar. He writes, "Babaji had applied to university for recognition of his college. A team of inspectors from the university was likely to visit the college. Some people advised him that it would be better to remove the photographs of R.S.S. founder, the late Dr. Hedgewar, and the then Sarasanghchalak Shri Guru ji from the auditorium of the college, temporarily, for the period of inspection. Babaji retorted, 'I do not care for the university-recognition. Photographs will not be removed.' Babaji was a strict disciplinarian. His college started at 6.30 a.m., and the doors were closed thereafter. Prescribed uniform was compulsory for students as well as teachers. Once Shri Madhukara Rao Chaudhary, the then Education Minister of Maharashtra, was scheduled to visit Babaji's college to offer some gifts at 3.30 p.m. The minister reached the college late; at 5 p.m. Babaji told him that the programme was over. Shri Chaudhary was a liberal person and did not get angry."

The college started with prayer at 6.30 a.m. Permission could be obtained to come to college up to 6.40 a.m. with a fine of four *annas*. No permission was granted after 6.40 a.m. Babaji was never late in the college. He had declared, "I will resign the post of Principal the day I am late in the college."

Shri Ratnaparkhi is a retired judge from Mumbai High Court. Earlier he was appointed as a lecturer to teach Economics in Babaji's college. He says, "Babaji was in jail during Emergency in the year 1975. His wife Mangala Tai's health deteriorated and she fell seriously ill. Her son was studying in Nasik and the married daughter was far away, so nobody was with her. A friend of Babaji sent a proposal to government that Babaji should be released on parole. Local Congress leaders too had no objection. I was an officer in the Law department of Maharashtra Government. The Law Minister called me and asked me about the legal implications of the parole. I told him, 'I will put forward the legal advice, but will the man you want to release on parole be ready for the parole?' Next day Law Minister told me, 'The man is not ready for release on parole.' I could imagine the steadfastness of Babaji that is why I had put the question to the Minister." The Nagpur University deputed another team to inspect the college. Some students had lodged some complaints. One of them was that it was compulsory in his college to recite the full script of *Vande Mataram*. A member of the team remarked, "It is a crime to recite the full script of Vande Mataram." Babaji retorted, "If reciting the full script of Vande Mataram is a crime then I will commit that crime daily. Please register the case. I will face the consequences."

It was decided to hold a training camp of R.S.S. Vidarbh *Prant* in Yavatmal. That time the Maharashtra Government had made a rule that no government-aided institution would provide any building or field for any R.S.S. programme. Babaji said that the R.S.S. programme would be held in his college building and on the college field. "Who is government to order me?" he commented. Two R.S.S. training camps took place in Yawatamala in Date College only during the years 1981 and 1982.

Yes, it was the Date College, as recognized by people, though its formal name was Vishuddha Mahavidyalaya. According to Western science of logic 'Proper Nouns have no connotation', but the Date College had attained a qualitative meaning. Date College meant a college that observed discipline, taught patriotism, made students and teachers contribute in labour (*Shramdan*), the college that provided forbearance and succour to poor students in crisis. The college had a boarding house. It was the only boarding house that provided lodge and food just for ₹ 220/- for one whole year.

Anyone will have to be wonder struck on knowing about the commitments Babaji prescribed with teaching in the college. He got some work done by anyone getting any amenity from him. He engaged such students in running the potato and onion shops. A flour mill, ice factory, and a citizens' cooperative bank were also established. In due course, he founded a women's cooperative bank run exclusively by women. There was a barren hill, about 3-4 kms from Yavatmal. Today it is lush green with about thirty thousand trees. All that has been possible because of the *Shramdan* contributed by himself and his students.

Dr. Jatakar's maternity house is there. A lady delivered there an illegitimate child. Someone phoned to Babaji that a Christian missionary was willing to take that child. So what should be done? Babaji replied immediately that he would take care of the child. That is how an orphanage called 'Maya Pakhar' started. Maya means parental affection, and Pakhar means shelter. That shelter of parental affection is functioning with the inspiration and management by Babaji even today. One of his students writes, "In the year 1960 I got admission in the Date College. After one year I thought I will have to discontinue my studies due to lack of resources. Babaji employed me as a part time worker with ₹ 20/- p.m. as remuneration. Thus, he enabled me to continue my studies. In the year 1964 I earned B.Com degree. I got job as a teacher, but I was not satisfied. I was eager to work like Babaji in my rural area. I resigned the job, and decided to open a school in my village. I needed rupees five thousand urgently, so I went to Babaji. Immediately he spoke to manager of the Urban Cooperative Bank, and I got the money same day. My school started. Babaji gave half a truck of furniture for the school. When I purchased land for constructing the school building Babaji helped me in getting loan from the same cooperative bank."

Now no more is the great man who was courageous enough to crush all hindrances, ever ready to face turmoil created by his opponents, stable, unswerving, and gifted with fiery zeal, but with a conscience full of everlasting love and affection. A country becomes great due to such individuals, not due to the greedy running after power and pelf.

□

> *"Excellent are the persons who do good to others even at the cost of their own interests. Mediocre are the ones, who, while not opposing their own interests, do good to others. But the ones who harm others' interests for the sake of their own interests are devils in human form. We do not know how to define those who damage others' interests without any purpose."*
>
> **—Neeti Shatak**

15

SEWA DHAM VIDYA MANDIR

Last week The New York Times published an article about the Sewa Dham Vidya Mandir of Delhi, run by Sewa Bharati. Name of the writer indicates that she is an Indian, but the contents of the article indicate that she is a secular, i.e. hostile to Hindus, otherwise she would never have termed the good academic institution as a 'Madarsa'.

I have visited the Sewa Dham Vidya Mandir. The principal of the institution, in its initial stages, was my friend Vasant Rao Fadnavis of Vidarbha. To my knowledge, he and his wife worked in Sewa Dham for about three years. Where is this Sewa Dham? For whom was it opened? What type of education is imparted there? If we have correct information about these aspects, we may protect our mind from being poisoned by the biased and polluted stuff published in *The New York Times*. One more relevant point. Ever fascinated to rejoice using used material, a Delhi-based English daily also published that article already published in *The New York Times*. The newspaper did not feel it necessary to depute its own reporter to visit the Sewa Dham Vidya Mandir and obtain correct information about the school.

It is well known that Sewa Bharati is an organisation devoted to service works, and it is conducted by the *Swayamsewaks* of R.S.S. Patronised by Sewa Bharati the Sewa Dham Vidya Mandir is situated in East Delhi, about two kms away from Mandoli village near Nand Nagri. It was founded in the year 1988. The motive behind founding this institute has been to impart good education to the children of the Scheduled Castes (SC) and Scheduled Tribes (ST). It is a known fact that normally people belonging to Scheduled Castes and Scheduled Tribes are poor. Providing good education in private educational institutions, which charge exorbitantly, is beyond the resources of the poor SC/ST people. These students do not belong to Delhi only. They are from distant states such as Assam, Jharkhand, Madhya Pradesh and Rajasthan, etc. So the institute has to provide them the required lodging, etc. It is a residential institution.

Sewa Dham is spread in a beautiful building built on the donated five acre land. It has 80 rooms, and a huge auditorium that can accommodate 1200 people. There is a well-organised kitchen, and a dining hall, where 400 persons can dine together. Three acre land is reserved as playground. Education is imparted from 6th to 12th class. It is affiliated with the CBSE, the Central Board for Secondary Education, which is a Central Government body. Students are prepared for examination by this board. There is a reading room, well furnished, for the students, having more than seven thousand books. There are laboratories for studies in Physics, Chemistry and Biology. Facilities like computer training and well-equipped health care centre are also provided in the school. There were 287 students in the session 2002, 121 of them were from Scheduled Tribes, 54 from Scheduled Castes,73 from other backward castes, and 30 from other communities. The Vidya Mandir has set certain specific goals for itself. It is essential to ensure due refinement in the working for providing free education and lodging facilities to students, therefore, the system comprises suitable programmes to develop physical, mental, intellectual and spiritual capacities. Programmes are held to inculcate and awaken sense of patriotism, self-respect, and dutifulness in students. Daily routine is strictly disciplined; so that the youngsters may become refined citizens, and attain strong will-power and steadfastness. There are some extraordinarily talented and noble-minded students among the lot. Such students are spotted and special arrangements are made for their further development.

Two hundred and fifty students appeared in class 10th examination from 1993 to 2001. All of them passed. One hundred and sixty-two out of them passed with 1st class. One hundred and eleven students appeared in 12th class examination from 1995 to 2001. All of them passed. Fifty-one out of them scored 1st class. Seven students of 12th class earned merit scholarship due to their special attainments in the examination conducted by the CBSE.

The Vidya Mandir is leading in the field of sports also. Seventy-five students had taken part in competitive display of physical activities held on all India basis. They won 37 gold medals, 27 silver medals, and 22 bronze medals. Information regarding where the SC/ST students went for further education after passing out 12th class is available in school. Twenty-five students got admission in engineering colleges, and eight scored seats in medical colleges. Seventy-six students joined degree colleges and eight joined Army. Five students joined teachers' training institutes, and two dedicated themselves in service activities. Others also scored remunerative jobs.

Annual expenditure on each student comes to ₹16,000/-. Thus, in the year 2001-02 there was expenditure of rupees forty-eight lakh. The Vidya Mandir does not take any government grant. Donors from society bear the expenses. Our friends in foreign countries also donate. There are various types of donations for willing donors. They may become monthly donors, adopt a student for education, gift textbooks and stationery, earn merit by donating ₹ 5000/- for one-time meal, and contribute in the pool of funds.

Refinement of character being the priority of the school, programmes related with *Yogic* education and *Sangh Shakha* are convened regularly. Whether calling such an institute, which prepares students for the examination conducted by government, a *Madarsa*, or an illegitimate institute, is infamy for the Vidya Mandir, or glory for *Madarsas*, is left for the readers to decide.

□

> *"As a black bee sucks nectar from a plant so should a ruler tax public. Cows should be milked with due consideration for her dependent calf. Cow nipples should not be twisted."*
>
> **—Mahabharat**

16

SOCIAL JUSTICE COURT

Solapur is the fourth largest city of Maharashtra, the largest being Mumbai, followed by Pune and Nagpur. It is adjacent to Karnataka on one side and Andhra Pradesh on the other, so there is a large number of Kannada- and Telugu-speaking people in the city. The handloom industry of Solapur is very famous for production of cotton sheets. It earns foreign currency also. The other big business in the city is that of *bidi* and cigarette, which employs mostly Telugu-speaking workers, women in a good number. Telugu-speaking workers face many problems, and to solve them they themselves have founded a Social Justice Court. It is an informal public court, which has been working for about 4-5 years. It has earned confidence of public because of its unbiased adjudications. It was founded with the remarkable initiative of Padmabai Mahanta and Vishnu Karampuri. About 1.5 lakh Telugu people in the city are divided in more than 50 castes. Padmabai Mahanta is a lady worker engaged in the field of social work. She says, "We have been busy for the last ten years in solving the problems of bidi and powerloom workers. We observed that women workers are exploited at places of their work, as well as their homes. We thought of doing something for them. In the meantime some women came to us with their family problems. I solved their problems, and they built their trust in me, and made up their mind that I could help them in any crisis. Then we opened a 'Complaints Redressal Centre.' The success of the centre transformed it into a 'Social Justice Court'. Now it has earned recognition by the police department as well as the Complaint Cell of the government. Usually, the women bidi workers face problems like beating by their drunkard husbands, wives leaving their husbands' homes, polygamy, adultery, rape and property disputes, etc. When such problems are reported to police, more complications proliferate rather than solution. So people approach us. We do not disclose their names, and charge them nothing. Every Wednesday and Sunday we sit from 10 a.m. to 4 p.m. to solve their problems. We take from them only written complaints, hear the concerned parties, and adjudicate. Our verdicts are accepted by all."

Ramchandra Midda, a recipient of justice from the Social Justice Court, says, "We got justice due to Karampuri and Padmabai. Now our family runs normally. I shall not tell you our problem, but the court has surely made us happier." A police constable said, "This court has eased our work. Now whenever we get a complaint we refer it to the Social Justice Court."

Obviously, when the disputes like the ones mentioned above are reduced, then only it will be possible to say that our society has been reformed.

□

> *"Pacification of fire is possible by water. An intoxicated elephant can be pacified by a sharp iron hook. An ailment can be pacified by medicines. Poison can be pacified by applying Mantras. Our scriptures have remedies of all kinds, but there is no medicine for stupidity."*
>
> **—Neeti Shataka**

17

NIRU LANTERN

Anil Rajvanshi is name of a man who has been awarded the prestigious Jamna Das Bajaj Award for his contribution in development of villages. After attaining master degree in Mechanical Engineering from IIT Kanpur, he did research work in Solar Energy in Florida University of America, and earned doctorate. He taught in the university for about two and a half years. His wife, Nandini, also earned doctorate degree from the same university in Agriculture Science. Eighty-five thousand scholars have earned doctorate degrees from this university in different fields. The university decided to select out of them the most creative citizens and reward them. For the selection, they constituted a committee of twenty members, which included senior officers from Clinton administration, and Judges from the Supreme Court of America. The august committee selected 47 citizens for the prestigious award. Nandini Rajvanshi was one of them. She was the only one expert from outside America, who earned the award.

In 1981, the Rajvanshi couple left America and returned to India. Back home, they could score highly remunerative and prestigious jobs in accordance with their ability and academic attainments. They got some suitable offers also, but they ignored all those lucrative appointments of high salary and decided to dedicate themselves in the field of rural development. Nandini's father had an institute called 'Nimbakar Agricultural Research Institute', which is situated in Faltan city, about 100 km from Pune. Both of them joined the institute, and started thinking on what should be done for the rural farmers. The famous Nimbakara Seed is the product of this institute. While working there Anil Rajvanshi invented a novel lantern, which can give illumination equal to what a hundred watt electric bulb gives. This lantern can function with any of the fuels like ethanol, diesel or kerosene. Fuel consumption in this lantern is 60% less than what a petro max of the same wattage consumes. The lantern can also be used in emergency in kitchen as a stove. The lantern is named after the name of the couple's daughter, Niru. It took four to five years in conceiving the idea, research, and then production of the 'Niru Lantern.' Problem of distribution followed the production. Advertisements appeared in prominent newspapers, but there was no expected response. However, there was good response after they advertised with photograph of the lantern on Internet website, maximum from the state of California, America. Its sale got a boost. California was badly hit by frequent power cuts because of the Enron scandal, so people of California felt the need of Niru Lantern. It was a matter of pride for India that the lantern invented for her rural areas illuminated California. Another invention and production of Anil Rajvanshi was a novel type of rickshaw, which proved to be a great relief to labour class. How a common rickshaw-puller toils and gasps on ascents and gets drenched in sweat is well known. The poor from U.P. and Bihar opt for rickshaw pulling in big cities, and often fall victim to tuberculosis. It is said that cycle rickshaw was introduced in our country in the year 1920, but no efforts were made to improve its functioning before Anil Rajvanshi's invention, which brought mechanical improvements in rickshaw. He provided three gears, brake to rear wheels, good aerodynamics and comfortable seat for driver. This invention too, like the Niru Lantern, was ignored in India. Internet website helped. There were enquiries from Europe and America. Some rickshaws were sold. The Pidi Cab Company of London purchased four rickshaws, which are hired by tourists to visit the city of London. Production may increase if the London experiment succeeds. It is regrettable that in spite of our indigenous efficiency for innovative developments we keep on expecting from foreign countries. How can the country become great with such trends? Country can become great due to the talents of its own people. The Rajvanshi couple has set an example.

☐

"There should be no doubt in deciding whether circumstances create a leader, or a leader creates circumstances. It is a leader who creates circumstances."

—A proverb

18

FRAGRANCE OF HUMANISM

Partavada is the name of a city situated at a slope of Satpura hills. Now it has become a tehsil in district Amarawati. Earlier, during British days, it was part of Achalapura tehsil and Achalapura cantonment. Vajjhar is the name of a village situated about 15 km from Partavada. I went to that village on 16 April 2000. No habitation was visible; I saw a hill nearby with trees having no leaves. The dryness of the hill appeared to be drier because of the scorching Sun. There was no possibility of any harvest. The stones all around would warn immediately anyone willing to grow some crops there, "Desist from harvesting here. It is no place for that. Leave us alone as we are." However, Shankar Papalkar harvested there, not cereals, not vegetables, not fruits, but service for humanity. Gardens spread fragrance of flowers and fruits. These hills, having no greenery, spread fragrance of humanism.

Shankar Papalkar told me that he had purchased 25-acre hills. I thought he must be a fool. We went forward, and saw a two-room small house. The house displayed a board with inscription, '*Atal Bihari Vajpayee Adivasi Niwasi Matimand Vidyalaya, Mukkam Vajjhar*'. It was a residential school for the mentally retarded aborigines who lived there, named after Shri Atal Bihari Vajpeyi. I was surprized. I knew that Shankar Papalkar was no BJP worker. He had canvassed always for Congress candidates. I asked him, "Had you taken permission from Vajpayee before naming your school?" He replied, "No. I feel Vajpayee is a great man, so I used his name."

I knew Shankar Papalkar for the last about 17-18 years. Once, when I went to Achalapura, Shankar had taken me to his home. It was night. Though I could not see the house properly, it did reflect all signs of poverty. Shankar was born in caste dhobi, but he is not shy. Shankar was born in the dynasty of Sant Gadge Maharaj, the famous saint of Maharashtra, who was praised profusely even by Dr. Baba Saheb Ambedkar.

Shankar Papalkar is illiterate. He pronounces "Mook Badhir", meaning dumb and deaf, as "Mukh Badhir", which is the name of his project to serve the dumb and deaf. He is editor of a monthly magazine. It is not necessary that an editor should know reading and writing. He obtains articles from writers and publishes a good magazine. Nobody knows whether he remains barefoot always, without any footwear, but everyone accepts the fact that his feet are never stable. He keeps on moving as if some wheels are fixed under his feet. "Charaiveti" is the preaching of the *Vedas*. I firmly believe that Shankar Papalkar has never even seen the *Vedas*, keep aside the thought of his having read them, but he is devoted to conduct based upon preaching of the *Vedas*. I was present in a programme of his Mook Badhir School. I was surprized, and glad also, to see his work.

I do not know the source of his inspiration to toil for the service project. Keeping in view his property and resources (truly speaking, lack of them), it appears that his inspiration is inborn. The radiance of fire is only inborn. Does fire borrow radiance from someone? Shankar Papalkar is a self-motivated worker. His motivating pains are inborn. His hard works are self-motivated.

We reached Vajjhar on 16 April 2000 at 9 a.m. We were welcome by students of Papalkar's school for dumb and deaf with rhythmic beats of drums and *lezims*. I was supposed to do the *Bhoomi-Poojan* of the land earmarked for construction of a building for 'Apang Mahila Sudhar Griha' (Centre for amelioration of the handicapped women). That formality was completed. As usual, there were lectures, but I was anguished to see the condition of boys and girls present over there. On hearing their detailed description, I felt like weeping silently. My seniority in age forbade me from weeping openly and publicly, even from shedding tears. The services rendered by Shankar Papalkar are really hard *Tapasya*, penance, before which even a stone-hearted person will bow down reverentially. Who were those children? Some of them were the children recovered from gutters, where they were thrown by their own mothers, because they were illegitimate infants. Some of them were delinquents. Some of them were deserters from remand homes. None of them knew about their father or mother. Shankar Papallkar himself became their parents. Shankar shared with me some of his memoirs. A girl named Shailja was deaf and dumb. She was thrown into gutter and recovered to live in remand home. Shankar adopted her. He knew that uteruses of girls of 18-year age are removed by surgery in remand homes. It was not acceptable to Shankar. He decided to educate the girl in his Mook Badhir School, and get her settled in life. She passed 4th class, and serves the school as a peon. Shailja is now married. The district collector of Amarawati did her *Kanyadan*. There are so many girls and boys who get Shankar's fatherly affection. I met at least ten children who told me that Shankar was their father. According to tradition in Maharashtra, name of a person comprises his or her father's name also, first being the person's name and the second the father's name.

Accordingly, children told their names as 'Zebunnisa Shankar Papalkar', 'Mohammad Shankar Papalkar', 'Roli Shankar Papalkar', 'Pandurang Shankar Papalkar', all belonging to different communities, such as Hindu, Muslim and Christian. It appeared that those children represented all the destitute, orphan, and handicapped ones of whole India, assembled in Vajjhar, and Shankar had accepted them under his benign compassion. He attained the fatherly patronage through a court of Law. Shankar is Hindu. He did not change names of the children coming from different backgrounds. The number of mentally-retarded students in his school has reached 63. Boys and girls were standing on both sides of the path on which we were passing. Shankar called a boy aged about 10 or 12 through gesture, straightened his hand from elbow to wrist, and gave 7-8 heavy fist-blows with full strength on the hand. I was stunned. I thought Shankar was behaving like a devil. The boy betrayed no sign of pain. Shankar told me that the boy had lost all sensibility. He was a benumbed living human.

We proceeded towards dining hall of the hostel. We saw a girl, who, as Shankar told us, eats twenty *rotis* in one sitting; even then her appetite is not satiated. She eats even excreta and dung. She eats pebbles like betel nuts. I approached her. She was eating pebbles. She opened her mouth, which was filled with soil. Papalkar asked a maid to get the girl's mouth cleaned. The maid told us that the girl, aged about 15-16 years, behaved like a child of 3-4 years. It was time for lunch, so all of us sat for *bhojan*. We were served rice, *daal*, and *roti*. Shankar brought a boy to me. Both his hands were missing. Shankar asked me to put a morsel of rice in the boy's mouth. Shankar opened his mouth, and I fed him a morsel of rice and *daal*. The sense of happiness that I noted on the boy's face made me feel as if I got the *Punya* of giving *Anna-Daana* to one thousand people. My eyes were filled with tears. Up to this date I have not been able to answer the question whether those tears were the outcome of pleasure, or of pain.

□

"Firstly, milk gave all of its qualities to water inherent in itself. When water saw the heat caused to milk, it sacrificed itself in the heat. When milk saw its friend, water, in trouble, it also rose up to jump into fire. It was pacified only on meeting its friend, water, again. Friendship of good people goes like that only."

—Neeti Shataka

19

BHAGAVADGITA IN TIHAR JAIL

I had heard the name of Tihar Jail of Delhi, but never seen it. I got the opportunity to see it on 30 November 2000. By the way, going to jail is not something special to me. I went to jail twice. Firstly, in the year 1948, when the R.S.S. was banned, I was imprisoned for participating in the Satyagrah Movement to oppose the ban. In the year 1975, I was imprisoned under MISA during the Emergency for 17 months. I suffered both of the jail terms in the Central Jail of Nagpur. I had never seen the Tihar Jail earlier. Having been imprisoned twice, I knew about the atmosphere of a jail, prisoners, food served to them, nature and behaviour of jail officials. So going to jail was not something new to me.

However, my visit to Tihar Jail on 30 November 2000 was caused by a different reason, not as a prisoner to suffer jail term. I was invited to visit it, and the invitation came from Shri Ram Krishna Goswami. Shri Goswami is no jail official, even then he invited me, and I accepted the invitation. Who is this Ram Krishna Goswami? He is a follower of *Shrimad Bhagavad Gita*. He is devoted to the mission of character building through the preaching of *Gita*, and he teaches the preaching to prisoners in jail. Once he came to me, and told about his mission. I was surprised and stunned for a while. *Bhagavad Gita*, and that too in a jail? My mind was not ready to find unison between the two, and then I recollected the fact that the preacher of *Shrimad Bhagavad Gita* to Arjun was himself born in jail, so there is a relationship between jail and the *Gita*. I do not know the place Shri Ram Krishna Goswami belongs to. May be, he is from Rajasthan or Uttar Pradesh. He hates bad customs, bad traditions, crime and exploitation. He wants to abolish all those evils, but he has no brave colleagues to fight with him, as if the whole society is full of cowards, hence tolerates insults. There are some courageous people in society, but their courage often turns into misadventure, and they suffer jail terms. Can their strength and courage be used for social weal? It was such a thought that attracted Goswami ji to Tihar Jail. Tihar is the biggest jail in Asia, full of hindrances, such as old rules of government and their strict compliance by jail officials. There remain huge possibilities of raise of many eyebrows on hearing the name of *Shrimad Bhagavad Gita* in the so-called secular State. Goswami ji is skilled in his mission, which is named as 'Aparadh Mukti Vaicharik Kranti Abhiyan', i.e. campaign to evolve ideological revolution, and liberation from crime. He met the jail officials and convinced them that he could liberate prisoners from criminal disposition by giving them good thoughts. All that was required was permission to meet prisoners. It was his good luck, and good luck of the prisoners, that he got permission to meet prisoners.

Shri Goswami is a staunch devotee of Shri Krishna. On meeting anyone he does not greet with *Namaste*, or Ram-Ram. He greets with the words 'Jaya Shri Krishna', reminding one of *the Gita*. It teaches how to live life. It is the firm conviction of Goswami ji that the *Gita* transforms the very course of one's life, provided its meaning is understood and preaching is settled in mind. It is his belief that enabled the *Gita* enter the jail.

I met many types of prisoners in the jail, educated and uneducated, from so-called high castes and low castes. Nobody delights journey to jail, and all of them had different reasons for imprisonment. Some of them had committed murders out of pangs of vehemence, some had committed theft because of some difficulties, some had committed misconduct under the influence of lust, and some had done swindling for quick money. No prisoner was proud of his doings that resulted in imprisonment. All of them were worried about what they will do after their release. They could imagine that society would not easily accept their existence with benevolence. They had the inkling that fingers will be raised towards them in any case of crime anywhere. Goswami ji touched this very aspect of their complexed mentality, so he built his influence on the prisoners on the basis of Shloka no. 30 of Chapter 9 of the *Gita*, which, quoting *Bhagwan* Shri Krishna, assures, "Even if the vilest sinner worships me with exclusive devotion, he should be accounted a saint; for he has rightly resolved." ("He is positive in his belief that there is nothing like devoted worship of God." The English translation of this *Shloka* has been quoted from the *Shrimad Bhagavad Gita* published by the Gita Press, Gorakhpur.) The *Sankeertan-Bhajan* of God does not mean only chanting His name. *Bhagavad Gita* means putting into practice the preaching enshrined in it. *Bhagwan* Shri Krishna says that any misconduct in life does not mean that one's whole life will be full of misconducts. Arrogance of committing crime will not be built if one realizes the fact that the crime was just an accident. Can any body aspire to become a wicked person? *Bhagavad Gita* says that criminals too are entitled to live good life. A criminal is free to renounce misconduct and become a righteous person, if he so desires.

Shri Goswami ji got entry not only to the barracks of the prisoners, but to their minds also, on the basis of this Divine Assurance. He sent for the *Gita* books in bold texts from the Gita Press Gorakhpur. Avoiding the text in Sanskrit, he read only the translation in Hindi, and preached accordingly. Number of the prisoners in his audience increased gradually. The literate among them started reading *Gita* themselves. One of the prisoners, a Dalit, started preaching. The other prisoners were so impressed by the preaching of that Dalit prisoner that they touched even his feet.

At 3.30 p.m. on 30 of November 2000 I reached Tihar Jail with Shri Goswami ji and my colleague Shri Kishor Kant ji. There was no difficulty in entering the jail as we were accompanied by Goswami ji. We reached a ward where 70-80 prisoners were present. Within no time, the number doubled. A prisoner read the Hindi translation of the *Shlokas* of Chapter 8 of the *Gita*. Goswami ji preached on the subject. I also spoke for 10 minutes. Then the prisoners narrated their experiences of change they gained in life after reading the *Gita*. A prisoner, who was under trial for a murder, said that he had not committed the murder so *Bhagwan Shri Krishna* would surely acquit him. "I have had this feeling, because the government witnesses are saying that they had not seen anything. It is all the grace of the *Gita*", he said. Three-four other prisoners also spoke. Their language suggested that they were educated, but criminals. The *Tapashcharya* of Shri Goswami ji has now started bearing fruits. On 25th of December a *Mahayajna* was convened. It was named as '*Rashtriya Suraksha Mahayajna*'. That year the *Gita Jayanti* was on 7th of December. Goswami ji asked the prisoners to start reading, hearing, and brooding upon one chapter of the *Gita* daily from that day. Prisoners accepted the proposal. This *Jnana Yajna* continued for 18 days. It was closed after the *Maha Yajna* on 25 December. The closing ceremony was held in the august presence of Smt. Mridula Sinha, the president of the Central Social Welfare Board. Four-five prisoners expressed their experiences. One of them said, "*Gita* is a great mantra, the instrument of thought, to save youth from crime." The other said, "I am highly educated. The materialistic social atmosphere made me go astray. *Gita* has put me on the right track." The third one said, "I was under pressure of crime when I came to jail. I had lost hope for life. My eyes were opened when I came in touch with the *Gita*. It is in the hands of God to give life, but to live life is in the hands of humans." The remarkable point was that the 187 prisoners who participated in the *Maha Yajna* declared on oath that they will not commit any crime in future.

The fragrance of fame of Shri Ram Krishna Goswami has reached up to Jammu Kashmir. A senior jail officer of J&K invited him. For three days, Shri Goswami delivered sermons on *Gita* to the prisoners of Jammu Jail. That jail officer was a Muslim. *Gita* belongs to all.

□

> *"You have the right to work, but never the fruit of work. You should never engage in action for the sake of reward, nor should you long for inaction. Perform work in this world, Arjuna, as a man established within himself, without selfish attachments, and alike in success and defeat."*
>
> —**Shrimad Bhagavad Gita**

20

VIDYA BHARATI

What is "Vidya Bharati"? Its name suggests that it is an institution connected with learning and education. It is not only an institution; it is a developing revolution, which started in the year 1952 as Saraswati Shishu Mandir in Gorakhpur. Now this flow of knowledge, like the pious Ganga ji, has spread throughout India. Brought by Bhagirath from Swarg, Gangaji provided redemption to sixty thousand sons of Maharaj Sagar. The flow of the Vidya Bharati, it may well be called Vidya Bhagirathi, is geared up to provide new life to millions of students. There are so many sub-flows and rivulets that have branched out of Vidya Bharati. It has caused an indelible effect in the field of education. Vidya Bharati is growing, and it aspires to grow further. It is capable to keep on growing.

In 1952, there was only one Shishu Mandir. Today the number of the institutions affiliated with *Vidya Bharati* is 18,749. The number of the teachers in these institutions is 98,700. Total number of students is twenty-four lakh, two thousand, six hundred and twenty-nine. Details of the 18,749 educational institutions are as follows: Urban schools – 6,719, rural schools – 9,667, schools for forest dweller students – 1,398, primary schools – 8,918, middle schools – 2,536, high schools – 1,189, higher secondary schools – 447, colleges – 13, educational colleges – 17, technical schools – 9, vocational schools – 5, Ekala

Shiksha Vidyalaya – 1,579, Sanskar Kendras – 2,158, girls schools – 161, residential schools – 119.

As I mentioned above, Vidya Bharati is spread all over the country. All states, right from Ladakh to Andaman, have got schools of Vidya Bharati. Leh of Ladakh has a Vidya Bharati school on the bank of holy river Sindhu, which is known as 'Bharati Vidyaniketan'. It was started in the year 1999. In the West, Kutch has got a Vidya Bharati school. 80% of the students of this school are Muslims. It is no exception. The number of the Muslim students studying in various Vidya Bharati institutions is more than 65,000. We know that the worst hit area of Gujarat State, due to earthquake in the year 2000, was Kutch. Everything was destroyed due to the earthquake. School buildings were demolished, then Vidya Bharati started mobile schools, the Chal-Vidyalayas. The mobile school vehicle went to two villages daily for three hours in each village and imparted education to the children of 5 to 14 years age. Where did the students sit? In a temple, under a tree, in some one's room or wherever space was available. The vehicle went to a village thrice a week. Two vehicles are still commissioned on the work.

In the East, Vidya Bharati schools were opened in Assam two decades ago, benefitting students from 700 tribes. In Haflang, a school was started in two huts. Now, with public cooperation, the school has got a grand building. All activities of Vidya Bharati run on the cooperation and support of public only, as it does not take any grant from the government.

In the South, Saraswati Vidya Mandir started in 1985 in the group of islands in Port Blair (Andaman & Nicobar). Two more schools are running at other places. The school in Port Blair imparts education up to 8th class.

What is so special about the Vidya Bharati schools? One speciality, as mentioned above, is that they do not take any government grant, so they are not tied by any network of bureaucratic rules and regulations. Since the students have to be equipped for the examinations prescribed and controlled by government, they have to study curriculum as laid down by the government boards of education. The results of examinations in the schools run by Vidya Bharati are quite commendable. Last year, seven out of the first ten students who topped the quality test of examinations conducted by Madhya Pradesh Board of Education, seven students were from schools affiliated to Vidya Bharati. In 12th class examination, five out of the ten toppers belonged to Vidya Bharati schools. There has never been any difficulty in getting students for the schools, because of their track record and reputation of excellent results in common examinations. There has never been difficulty in getting students, but there has always been difficulty in selecting them out of the lot aspiring to get admission.

In my view, the most important and special trait of the Vidya Bharati schools is that they do not subscribe to the notion that preparing students for examinations is the only responsibility of schools. They impart further education. They teach *Yoga*, Sanskrit language, music, and through them they teach *Bharatiyata* and nationalism. Late Shri Lajja Ram Tomar, the former organising secretary and *Marg Darshak* of Vidya Bharati said, "The priority number one of the British regime was to ensure complete obliteration of the flourishing system of Bharatiya education. They replaced the spiritual culture and the spiritual life-structure and style, which was the very soul of Bharatiya education, with the Western philosophy of materialism. They installed and established pseudo, imitative lifestyle in our education system. This flawed education system was criticised everywhere after Independence. No darkness can be removed merely by cursing it. What becomes obligatory is kindling a lamp. It was with this inspiration that the Swayamsevaks of the

R.S.S. founded the Saraswati Shishu Mandir in the year 1952 in Gorakhpur."

While explaining the original difference between students of the schools affiliated with Vidya Bharati and other common schools, Shri Tomar said, "In Vidya Bharati schools emphasis is made on the aspect of refinement of character along with imparting education in traditional subjects. The biggest flaw of modern education system is that it is limited within the realm of scholarship only. It does not enter the arena of attitude building. In Vidya Bharati schools, emphasis is made on balancing development of both, scholarship and mental attitude. Students of Vidya Bharati are imbued, attitudinally, with the Sanskars of Bharatiya Sanskriti, patriotism and social sensitiveness. Simultaneously, they never lag behind in any field of knowledge."

The attitudinal education imparted in the schools of Vidya Bharati is denounced by the pseudo-secularists as 'saffronisation'. I think, the word saffronisation is not a condemnable word. It denotes very special qualities, attributes and virtues. It is indicative of sacrifice, dedication and lofty character. That is why saffron flag is hoisted on each holy temple. Saffron coloured is the robe of the *Sanyasis*. The secularists know neither their culture nor their value system. I pity their ignorance. I have given in this book some reference of the education system prevailing for the students of the SC/ST categories in Delhi-based Sewa Dham. An American journalist saw it and described the school as Hindu *madarsa*. That journalist knows neither the meaning of the word Hindu, nor does he understand a *madarsa*. His ignorance too is pitiable. His sources of information, ultimately, are the news items published in big English newspapers. Such journalists have neither time nor capacity to reach the roots of the news, but such scandalous propagandas cannot stop the progress of Vidya Bharati. It is bound to advance. Its progressive journey of fifty years cannot make it sit with inertia and smugness. It is resolving to set new goals under the auspices of its golden jubilee.

□

> *"May cows yield plenty of milk. May the Earth be prosperous with all kinds of food grains. May there be timely rains, and breeze blow to give bliss to all. May all living beings be happy. May the learned people with fine conduct be honoured always, and may dutiful and respected kings competent to suppress enemies rule the Earth."*
>
> **—Mrichchha Katikam**

21

A SAGE OF LEARNING

Pandit Vasant Tryambak Shevde passed away in Kashi on July 5, 1999. I was extremely sad to know of his demise, because that day I was in Sarnath, a nearby township, still I could not have his last *darshan*. There was a meeting of the *Karyakari Mandal* of R.S.S. in Sarnath. The meeting was over on 6 July after lunch. Train for Nagpur was scheduled late night. I had made up my mind earlier to return to Nagpur only after meeting Vasant Rao Shevde. He lived in Ghasitola locality of Kashi. When I was preparing to go to Ghasitola, a *Swayamsevak* of Ghasitola informed me that Shevde ji had expired a day earlier. I was stunned to hear the sad news, and recalled the adage, "*Ishwarechchha Baliyasi*." The whole screen of episodes of memories appeared on my mind.

Pure Worship of Knowledge

Vasant Rao expired in Kashi, though he did not belong to Kashi. His whole education and training was accomplished in Nagpur. Nagpur was then the capital of the province of C.P. and Berar, and there was a famous college called Maurice College. After my matriculation when I took admission in that college Vasant Tryambak Shevde was a student in that college. He attained M.A. in Sanskrit. He passed away in 1999. What did he do during the period of 58 years? He only worshipped knowledge, and nothing else. He did not get married, nor did he ever serve to make money. Indeed, he did serve Bhagavati Saraswati. Yes, it was a service. Like a devoted and punctual service person, who attends office from 11 a.m. to 5 p.m., Vasant Rao Shevde devoted his great perseverance in pursuit of knowledge from 11 a.m. to 5 p.m. The only difference was that while a common service person observed Sunday as holiday, Vasant Rao did not take leave from the service of *Devi Saraswati* even on Sundays. That was his unparalleled devotion.

Daily morning he worshipped Bhagawati Durga. I happened to meet him once casually in Nagpur. He invited me to his new house in Lakshmi Nagar locality. I asked him whether he had got married. He replied, "I could not spot any lady as beautiful as Devi Durga. The pledge that I had vowed is continuing: propitiation of Bhagawati Durga and adoration of Bhagawati Saraswati." During mornings he kept himself busy in the worship of *Durga*, and after a meal studied from 11 a.m. to 5 p.m. to adore *Saraswati*. During nights he read some '*light stuff*'. What was the light stuff? Reading of original documents of Maratha history, and before sleeping, memorising the Sanskrit lexicon committed to memory earlier. Such was his supernatural penance for knowledge during the 58 years. The atmosphere at his residence was not appropriate for such type of penance for knowledge. It was quite incongruous. His father, Shri Tryambak Rao alias Shri Dada Saheb Shevde, was a famous legal expert of Nagpur. That time, during British rule, he was Advocate General. Eventually, he became a judge in Nagpur High Court. Dada Saheb was a handsome man, an impressive orator, and a worshipper of beauty. I had not seen the mother of Vasant Rao ji, but seen his step mother. She was a tennis player. The atmosphere of his house, in the decade of 1940, was most modern. Elder brother of Vasant Rao had gone to study in England after passing 8th class, not because there was no arrangement after 8th class in Nagpur. It was just to let the world know that Dada Saheb's son had gone to study in England. He completed his education there only, married an English woman, and unfortunately passed away there only in young age.

The outward appearance of the house reflected liking for enjoyment of aesthetics and poetry. Beautiful ladies frequented the house often. Snehprabha Pradhan, the well-known film actress of those days, stayed at Shevde ji's residence whenever she came to Nagpur. One room of the same house, however, was never ready to allow entry to beauty or modernity. Wooden dumbbells were kept in a corner of the room for physical exercise. There was an iron bed, and almirahs full of books. Floor of the room was covered with carpet. This room belonged to Vasant Rao Shevde. Once he told me in jest, "The guests visiting our house think that I am cook of the house." Thus, two extremities of lifestyle existed together, simultaneously, in the same house.

My Guru

I had no special acquaintance with him till the year 1944. His attire distinguished him from other students. He wore a round black cap, head completely shaven. I never saw him going by car, although there were many cars at his residence. He used bicycle. His classmates told me that he put off his cap as soon as he sat in his class room, wiped sweat on his skull with a white handkerchief, and put on the cap again. Few college-going students wore caps those days, so Vasant Rao attracted attention instinctively.

I passed B.A. examination in 1944, and attained gold medal from the university for scoring highest marks in Sanskrit. I wanted to do M.A. in English literature, and aspired, simultaneously, to score the King Edward Memorial Scholarship, which, in those days was supposed to be a very prestigious award. In English, I had scored 3 marks less than the required 60%, the criterion to attain the award. So I decided to do M.A. in Sanskrit, and attained that prestigious scholarship. Though I had attained first position in Sanskrit in B.A., my knowledge of Sanskrit was not of the high standard that I aspired. So I decided to indulge in original study of Sanskrit with Vasant Rao Shevde. I requested him to teach me Sanskrit. Very politely he said, "I do not possess the required ability to teach someone, still if you wish, you are welcome, we shall study together." Daily, after my classes were over in the college, I went to his residence. He read, and I heard. Though he too had learned Sanskrit only through English medium, he was not satisfied with that. He had learned grammar from Shri Vasudev Shastri, a specialist in *Vyakaran Shastra.* Eventually, he developed his knowledge by dint of his own hard work. He never appeared in any competitive examination, because he had no desire to get any worldly honour or job. He would have become a *Vyakaranacharya* easily had he appeared in any examination. While busy in the process of research in the bottom of the ocean of *Vyakaran Shastra*, he wanted to study the *Nyaya Shastra* also. So he took elementary lessons in that field from my predecessor, Shri Bapat, who was a teacher. In due course, like Ekalavya, he persevered himself, and became a pundit of the *Nyaya Shastra.* His father wanted him to attain degree in Law from the law college, and practise law. When Vasant Rao did not accept the proposal, he was advised to go to Germany for higher studies in Sanskrit. Vasant Rao felt that the facilities for higher studies in Sanskrit available in our country existed nowhere else. After a few years, when two German students started coming to him to learn the *Nyaya Shastra*, everybody appreciated his high standards of knowledge. I studied with him *Tarkbhasha*, and the topics of *Sandhi* and *Krudanta* of *Siddhant Kaumudi*. That is how I attained a little bit of fundamentals of Sanskrit. I came to know how to comprehend the *Balmanorama,* and meaning of *Mallinatha's* explanations and commentaries on various classical works. I could know the original definition of *Nyaya Shastra*. It was an end to my tendency of being satisfied with superficial information, and my mind was inclined to comprehend the fundamentals. I am indebted to him for my whole life for this new vision.

I stood first in university in M.A. also, and scored the gold medal. He wanted me to indulge in deep study of *Nyaya Shastra*, but I had resolved not to become a scholar. ("Why had you resolved not to become a scholar"? The translator asked Shri M.G. Vaidya while translating this book into English. His short reply was, "Because of the Sangh Karya"). "That made Shevde ji a little upset, but his affection for me remained intact."

A Genius Like Kalidas

Usually, the pundits of *Vyakaran* and *Nyaya* are taken as blunt and rough. They are often busy in discussing *ghata* (pot, or capability) and *pata* (clothing, or exterior aspects). Vasant Rao was an exception. He was a connoisseur, rich in aesthetic language. It may appear to be hyperbolic praise for him if we compare him with Kalidas, but I aver that nobody will doubt if any portion of his work is presented, without disclosing poet's (his) name, and ascribed it to Kalidas. Easily comprehensible language, flawless creation, shrewdness in avoiding even the slightest mistake of *Vyakaran*, all these attributes put together will mean Vasant Rao's poetry. His three great epics, *Vindhyavasini Vijaya, Sumbhavadha,* and *Devadeveshwar*; and the mini epics *Abhinava Meghdoot, Stav Manjoosha*, and *Raghunath Shiromani Charita* testify his erudite genius. *Vritta Manjari* was his first book. It is common to note a name in the characteristic features of a description, but the speciality with Vasant Rao is that even the illustrations of description indicate the name. Every illustration contains praise for Bhagawati Devi. What is the price of this book, the *Vritta Manjari*? No edition indicates any price. Every edition of the book mentions the price as '*Love*'.

Recognition Among the Erudite

His abilities were recognised when he left Nagpur, and went to Kashi, the abode of the mother of Sanskrit, where his abilities were evaluated. Vasant Rao was not only Vasant Rao. He became the "*Samasta Prachya-Pashchatya Vangmayam Karamalakekrutavan*" (the one who could view all the oriental and occidental literature like a man who views an *Amala* fruit, the Emblic Myrobalan, kept on his palm), "*Mahabhashyantam Vyakaranabhahina Krutyamiva Pratidianamanushelayan*", "*Vidyashevadhi*" and "*Bhasa-Kalidasa Bilhanadipratispardhe Kavivarenyah.*" He was honoured with the Sahitya Academy award also. He got a colleague like Dr. Brahmanand Tripathi, who looked after him during his old age. Apart from *Kavya*, he wrote books on *Nyaya* and *Vyakarana Shastra* also. His book on *Vyakarana Shastra*, titled "*Sphotatatvaniroopana*" was released in the month of February 1995 at Nagpur only. The people of Nagpur never saw him thereafter.

Infatuated by the supernatural beauty of Bhagawati Devi, this lifelong celibate really adhered to his vow of following the *Brahmacharya*. *Brahma* means knowledge, and he felt blessed in dedicating his whole life in pursuit of knowledge only. Once he told me, "God has not been just to me by giving me birth during this era." I do not agree with him, because the supernatural life of Vasant

Rao, devoted in pursuit of knowledge, brought him the bliss of blessedness.

It is such people who make the country great. That is why my Bharat is great.

□

> *"Love of goodness without love of learning degenerates into simple-mindedness. Love of knowledge without love of learning degenerates into utter lack of principle. Love of faithfulness without love of learning degenerates into injurious disregard of consequences. Love of uprightness without love of learning degenerates into harshness. Love of courage without love of learning degenerates into insubordination. Love of strong character without love of learning degenerates into mere recklessness.*
>
> **—Confucius**

22

INTERNATIONAL COOPERATION COUNCIL

'Antar Rashtriya Sahayog Parishad' (International Cooperative Council) is the name of an institution founded for maintaining mutual love, cordial relations and cooperation among the Indians living in foreign countries. Shri Baleshwar Agrawal (he is no more now) is the active chief worker of this council. Two crore Indians are living in 110 countries in six continents (in the year 2001). Shri Bhishm Kumar Agnihotri, who earned fame in Education department of America for many years, has been appointed by the government as an emigrant ambassador to look after the interests of Indians living in those countries (it was in the year 2001). The so-called secularists, or the anti-Hindu, newspapers created unnecessary ruckus on his appointment. Prior to that, Shri Agnihotri was the senior-most official of the Bharatiya Swayamsewak Sangh of America. Since the Bharatiya Swayamsewak Sangh is affiliated with R.S.S., the anti-Hindu newspapers got an opportunity to create hullaballoo.

Known as Non-Resident Indians (NRIs), most of these Hindus, these Indians have faith in India. They remember that they have come to these countries from India. They feel blessed when they get a chance to visit India, and fulfil their ambition to bathe in the holy rivers, visit the holy temples and make offerings to the holy places. Many students of foreign countries are getting education in Indian universities. Antar Rashtriya Sahayog Parishad organises meetings of such students. On 14 August 2002, the Parishad convened a gathering of newly-arrived foreign students at Hansraj College of Delhi University. The auspicious day of Independence was marked for the gathering. Shri Dani Lal Shiva, the Ambassador of Mauritius in India, and Professor A.S. Narang, the adviser to the students, were the chief guests at the gathering. Shri S. Arora, the Vice-Principal of Hansraj College presided over the programme. The Government of India has decided officially to establish cordial relations with Indians living in foreign countries. Manifestation of their decision will be observed on 9 to 11 January 2003 in the form of 'Pravasi Bharatiya Diwas'. The three-day convention will be inaugurated by the Prime Minister himself. The awardees of the Nobel and the Bharat Ratna, the highest awards, will appear together in the convention. It will also be attended by intellectuals, political leaders, social workers, prominent figures of commerce and industry, doctors, legal experts, writers, thinkers and artistes, who left their indelible footprints on various walks of life. That will be a peculiar world conference.

The deliberations will mainly cover, 'The role of the Indians scattered all over the world in the new millennium'; and 'The Report of Lakshmimal Singhavi Committee'. The Finance Minister, and the Foreign Minister of India will also address the meet. Chief Ministers of different states will be consulted about fiscal investments. It has been decided to observe officially 9th of January every year as 'Emigrant Indians Day'. 9th of January has its own justification and importance. It was on 9th of January (1915), when Mahatma Gandhi came to India from South Africa.

This convention will enable residents of India to get familiar with the sentiments of emigrant Indians. What has been their contribution to enrich their respective countries will come to light, and new doors will be opened for creation of some institutional initiatives. Everybody will be face-to-face with the greater India. There cannot be any reason to doubt that all these emigrants will get a very cordial reception from the people of India.

The Antar Rashtriya Sahayog Parishad has undertaken another initiative, construction of Emigrants' Building. The constitution of the Parishad, which was resolved in the year 1978 by the Parishad also mentioned that it would construct the building. Now, after 24 years that resolve is likely to get shape. The Urban Development Department of Government of India has allotted a 500 sqr mtr plot for that. The Parishad paid ₹ 10,86,613/- for the plot and got it on 6 May 2002. Now they are planning to construct a four, storied beautiful building, well furnished with all facilities. It will cost about one crore rupees. The Parishad hopes and believes that it would construct the building soon.

□

> *"May there be peace in the heavenly region. May there be peace in the atmosphere. May peace reign on the Earth. May the water be soothing and plants be source of peace to all. May all the enlightened persons bring peace to us. May the Vedas spread peace throughout the Universe. May all other objects give us peace and may peace even bring peace to all. May that peace come to us. Om Shanti, Shanti, Shanti."*
>
> —**Shanti Path Mantra**

23

JHANSI KI RANI, AND HER TANK

Well known is the name of Jhansi ki Rani. The city of Jhansi has attained immortality because of *Rani* Lakshmi Bai. There is a tank in that city, which is known as *Lakshmi Tal*. A few months earlier the condition of the tank was so miserable that the *Rani* of Jhansi, had she been alive and visited the tank, would have wept, and punished those who spoiled it. Now the condition of the tank is changed. Its filth has been cleaned, and it has become a tourist spot. This beautiful resting place of the *Rani* has become a pleasant and enjoyable spot again. This transformation has been done by Rajnish Dube, the magistrate of Jhansi. Is it the responsibility of a magistrate to clean and beautify a tank? No, but by doing a job beyond the scope of his laid down duties he earned extraordinary praise for himself, and added a feather to his cap.

Once Shri Dube was standing near the tank. A gust of wind brought him foul smell. It was from the water of the tank. It was natural, because about 200 year old tank contained all the dirty water released by the city through seven culverts, which added filth to the tank daily. Various types of vegetation had grown in the tank, which covered the water and raised the level of foul smell. Dube ji could not tolerate the foul smell, but he did not press his nose and run away. He decided to ameliorate the condition of the tank, and bring back its original beauty. Thus started the movement known as "Save the *Lakshmi Tal.*"

Magistrate is an administrative post, and in small cities the post carries a lot of commanding influence, but Shri Dube did not exploit his official position or government machinery. He took into confidence the public of the city. Everyone appreciated and supported his proposal to clean the tank. Businessmen, servicemen, tailors, fishermen, all joined hands and cooperated in the initiative. A seventy-year-old man stood for hours in the cold water to cooperate in the movement. Not a single rupee was spent from the exchequer. The local population afforded all the logistic support. Petrol pump owners provided petrol to run JCB machines, which extricated all the rubbish, waste material, mud and morass. Crasher Association provided tractors and trollies. Many voluntary associations provided food packets for the personnel engaged in the process of purification of the tank. The employees of Jhansi Development Authority gave one day's salary. Divisional Commissioner Smt Smriti Kakkar was also enthused. She arranged shirts printed with words, "*Lakshmi Tal Bachao*" (Save the *Lakshmi Tal*). When she went to the tank to distribute the shirts to volunteers, she saw that they were standing in knee deep mud.

For years the culverts and drains had been bringing dirty water and mud to the tank covered with vegetation. It was no easy task to remove all that filth, but the collective emotion and the high morale of the people accomplished the task within only three months. Face of the tank has been changed. Now people came to know why the *Rani* liked the tank. Now, if the *Rani* can come back to her old capital city, she will be extremely delighted to see her tank.

Nature has given too much to mankind. It has bestowed beauty, but man sullies this blessing given by Nature. When courageous men like Rajnish Dube, who derive pleasure from serving against current, come forward with determination, nature retrieves its naturally beautiful form. Really, unfortunate would be the person who does not commend the work done by Rajnish Dube.

□

> *"Cleanliness and order are not matters of instinct: they are matters of education, and like most great things, you must cultivate a taste for them."*
>
> **—Benjamin Disraeli**

24

MANGALA, A DALIT SARPANCH

Here is a story of a head woman elected in a village called Meghni in Madhubani region in Bihar State. The story is tinged with parallel agony, everlasting, for the woman. There were no *panchayat* elections in Bihar for 24 years, from 1978 to 2002. Elections took place after such a long period, and a young lady named Mangala was elected as *Sarpanch*, the head of the village council. Her courage and boldness are commendable. She belongs to the scheduled caste, so her reputation got wings.

The political atmosphere of Bihar has hardly been favourable to the idea of a lady contesting any election against a man. Mangala contested against men, and won, and created an example. However, the election was an acid test for her. Her beautiful and innocent face is bearing black scars of hurt. The only reason of the wounds was her audacity to fill up the election nomination form. It was because of that "crime" that her face was damaged by people. When she was being beaten, some people shouted, 'Crush the head of this female serpent, she has become mad'. They were scared and said, "If this chamaarin, (a lady from the scheduled caste), wins the election and becomes *mukhiya* (*sarpanch,* or a village head), she will make sure to urinate on our heads". People of Meghni had become crazy due to that 'fear', so they cracked her head smeared with blood. She fell unconscious.

The post of the *sarpanch* was neither reserved nor earmarked for any scheduled caste/tribe candidate. It was not earmarked for a lady candidate. A well-dressed man, a *babu saheb*, of the same village had filed nomination for the post on behalf of his veiled, purdah-observing wife, who stayed at home. The man's intention, obviously, was to work as the village head in the name of his wife. Not only that, the man had submitted his own nomination form for headship of a nearby village, so that he could have overwhelming influence on both of the villages. Mangala had challenged his ego. She had studied up to 10th class, but could not pass the examination because of her marriage. Conspiracies were being hatched to teach her a lesson since the day Mangala filed her nomination paper. Once her goat went astray and did not return till evening. So Mangala went out in search of the goat, a little away from her village. She was pried upon and attacked. Her hands that had filled up the nomination form were twisted, fingers pulled up and multiple injuries caused on her head. Normally, it is said, a wounded and blood smeared person gets scared, but the injuries suffered by Mangala emboldened her resolve and she became more courageous. She got necessary dressing, but did not go home. She went up to the village health centre, picketed and sat on fast there. She did not change even her blood-smeared clothes, hair undone and face bandaged. She proclaimed that she would not budge from there unless all the people of the scheduled castes and the scheduled tribes vote in her favour. For two days, she took only water and lemon juice. Her pure and nonviolent struggle, the *Satyagrah,* changed the village equations. Firstly, 30-40 people came and promised to work with her. Mangala said, "I will retaliate with votes on the people who attacked me with lathis. Injustice, in any form, will not be tolerated in this village." Mangala's husband is a peon in a rural institution. He stands behind his wife resolutely.

Mangala adopted a strategy, like a skilled politician. She declared that she would not go to court of Law against the attackers if she wins the election. "Ultimately, I too have to live in this village, but if I lose they will have to go to jail. I have full support of the police, I will name anyone of the village as attacker", she declared. This strategy worked for Mangala. The *babu saheb* withdrew his wife's candidature. Since Mangala belonged to a scheduled caste, the *babu saheb* played a trick. He decided to field two ladies of Mangala's community to oppose her. Initially, there was no consensus on their names, but finally two ladies also filed their nomination form, with the understanding that one of them will withdraw on the last day, and canvass for the other. Ultimately, Mangala won the election.

The soft-spoken and ever-smiling Mangala is not only a popular village head, she has changed condition of the village. Very discreetly, she did many commendable works within three months after she took over as a *sarpanch*. Some of the works she did are mentioned below:

- She managed cleanliness of the village and garbage disposal.
- She set right the employee of Primary Health Centre, who was irregular in his duties and sold in market the medicines meant for villagers. Mangala got two registers, one for marking his attendance, and the other for entry of receipt and distribution of medicines.
- She opened an Awareness Centre in the village, and encouraged the village women to start a bank for women. Bank accounts in post offices were closed and money transferred to the bank of the women. Within a few days a capital of ₹ 12,000/- was deposited. 10-12 families got financial aid as loan.

- Hitherto, agricultural labourers did not get the prescribed minimum wages, a practice not in vogue anywhere in Bihar. She convened many meetings of the village committee, discussed the issue, and a middle path was adopted. There was an increment of ₹ 10/- in the existing wages, and an understanding was evolved that the labourers would not demand the minimum wages for next two years.

The financial grant for the village never reached the village earlier. She wrote to the Development Officer and got success in managing the village funds and expenditure judiciously. Her opponents were wonder struck to see her management skill, discretion, and restraint she displayed in development of the village.

□

> *"An elephant has bulky body, but it is controlled by a goad. Is a goad as big as the elephant? Thunderbolt shatters mountains, is the thunderbolt similar to mountains? A lamp, when lit, destroys darkness, is darkness as small as the lamp? Oh! Brother, mighty is the one whose brilliance is sharp. What is there in hugeness of a shape?"*
>
> **—Adage**

25

BANK OF MOTHERS' MILK

We know and hear many things about blood donations and milk banks, but the second endeavour in whole India and the first in Gujarat is that of a bank of mothers' milk. The idea of milk bank was put forward by late Dr. B.C. Patel of Vadodara. He was inspired by the Milk Bank of Mumbai which had begun first. When Dr. Patel learned that many infants die due to lack of mother's milk, he found out the solution. He was the first founder and donor of the Mothers' Milk Bank. The Baroda Lions' Club helped quite a lot to further this initiative. This novel experiment was initiated in the year 2000 at the 'Kashibai Children Hospital' situated in Karelibag. The N.I.C.U. (Neonatal Intensive Care Unit) of this hospital for children admits the children born prematurely, sick children, and children with less weight, and gives them packed milk. Now with the establishment of the Mothers' Milk Bank this problem has been solved to a great extent.

The initiative comprises donor mothers of four types: the women who delivered recently may donate their spare milk after feeding their infants, the mothers who deliver in some other hospitals and their infants have to be kept in I.C.U. due to some reasons, such mothers are transferred from those hospitals to this hospital, the mothers who volunteer to donate their milk due to its affluence, and the working mothers of high classes of society. Milk is collected only after the mothers are fully convinced of the whole procedure of the bank.

Milk of the donor mothers is sucked with a pump made by a reputed firm, and collected in a steel pot. Its preservation process is completed within 24 hours. It is boiled for half an hour at 56°C. This process eliminates the bacteria and any virus of HIV. This process is called pasteurisation. The milk is then cooled, and stored at 20°C. This milk can be used up to three months.

There are two trained nurses for this work in Dr. Kashibai Hospital. Very skillfully and neatly they adhere to the laid down process, right from collecting the milk to preserving it, and distributing to the needy children. Fifty-one litre milk was collected and distributed to 240 infants in the year 2000. In 2001, it was 64 litre given to 338 infants, and in early 2002 it was 75 litre, given to 268 infants.

This work is getting popularity day by day. Initially, mothers hesitated, but now voluntary mothers are coming forward, unhesitatingly, Dr. Nirupama Munshi and Dr. Arun Pathak are also contributing to this initiative. According to doctors, the mortality rate of children can be minimised if this Gujarat born initiative is replicated throughout the country.

□

> *"It is now irrefutable that in absence of mom's own milk, donor milk increases survival rate and improves development of vulnerable infants."*
>
> **—Philly.com**

26

I.I.T. KANPUR STUNNED THE WORLD OF SCIENCE

The greatness of India is proved not by non-living objects, but by the perseverance and attainments of her people. Although from times immemorial the profound thinkers of *Bharat* have been ahead of all, yet their attainments in recent past have drawn attention of the scientists world over. Their achievements, even in the fields of mathematics and computer, all in the series of achievements of Param Computer and Cryogenic Engine, have brought immense reputation for India.

Indeed, a team of young scientists of the Indian Institute of Technology (I.I.T.), Kanpur, has stunned the international community of scientists. The readiness with which the Americans took their researches in Web Technology, and their far-reaching consequences, is really astonishing. Apparently, the research looks quite common. How to find whether a number is even or odd unit? It is easy to find in case of small numbers, but very difficult in cases of big numbers. For hundreds of years, mathematicians all over the world have been trying to find solution to this problem. Computer scientists also did their best to get the solution, but they failed. Indian scientists found the solution through their invention of world-level theoretical computer science. Manindra

Agrawal, Niraj Kayal and Nitin Saxena of I.I.T. Kanpur invented the Primality Algorithm, which gave the solution. This Algorithm enables one to know whether any number is divisible by any smaller number, or by 1, or by itself.

Manindra Agrawal, a 30-year-old research scholar, is a renowned scientist, well known in the international community of computer scientists. Niraj Kayal and Nitin Saxena, about 20-year-old research scholars, had achieved some part of the discovery of this unique algorithm while they were students of B.Tech. Whether a given number is divisible can be known through Primality Algorithm, but what is that dividing number cannot be known. If this invention is extended further to discover the dividing small number (it is known as 'Factorisation Algorithm') it would be possible to resolve the mysteries like the 'Security Codes' used in Credit Cards through computer programming. Thus, the whole electronic commerce industry will have to adopt the new security algorithm process.

Even prior to that Indian scientists have had remarkable attainments in theoretical computer science, but most of them have been working in foreign countries. Shri Madhusudan of M.I.T. has scored the Nevan Linna Award recently. This is the highest award of Computer Science, which was conferred upon him by the International Congress of Mathematicians in a convention held in Beijing. Among many of his inventions is the verifying process of algorithm, which is based on mathematical evidences. Developed with the cooperation of four other researchers, this algorithm system has been in vogue quite often. There are very negligible chances of its failure. As a result, chances of committing any mistake will be reduced gradually after the successive running of any given programme. Many years ago Mikel Robin had developed a similar logarithm, but it is because of the invention by I.I.T. Kanpur that there will be no chance of any mistake if this process is put to use regularly.

□

> *"Greatness lies not in owning resources, power, status or prestige. It lies in politeness, gentle demeanour, service and strength of character. Greatness is not in being powerful, it is in right application of power."*
>
> **—Adage**

27

GIFT OF BUDDHISM

There has been tremendous contribution of sages from various communities in making India adorable to the world. Very especial trait of grave thinkers of India has been the fact that to them all worldly things, including their body, has always been secondary to their pursuit of eternal knowledge for public well-being. *Bhagwan* Buddha himself was an example of that. Buddhism provided a great progression of such thinkers. Shri Yesheo was one of them. He was a very distinguished guru of the Buddhists of Ladakh and Tibet a thousand years ago. Yesheo had fought the Muslim invaders while pursuing his religious perseverance. Invaders imprisoned him. The Muslim commander demanded a particular amount of gold as ransom. Yesheo's followers managed the demanded gold for his release. When Yesheo came to know about the succession of events, he called some of his prominent followers and asked them not to give gold to the enemy. He said, "It would not be proper to lose so much gold just to save my life. I have become old, in any case. Use this wealth in furthering the cause of *Dhamma*. Today this stage has come because of the failure to appreciate the tenets of *Dhamma* and proper conduct based upon the tenets. Do not worry about me. Go to Vikram Shila Vihar located in Magadh state, and bring from there the great scholar called Acharya Dipankar Shri Gyan. His guidance will awaken the public, and *Dhamma* will develop. Faith of the people will be strengthened, and our whole society will become strong and powerful. Spend the gold only in the process of attainment of that great goal." Buddhists agreed, and followed his instructions. *Acharya* Dipankar Shri Gyan was brought. He was known as *Ateesh*. His incessant efforts brought new life in society, and the sovereignty of the Buddhists spread in the regions of Ladakh, Lahol and Speeti. Buddhists crossed swords, for about 300 years, with Muslim invaders, who invaded from the side of Kashgarh. That will for conquest persists in Buddhists even today. Organisations like the famous Ladakh Buddhist Association (L.B.A.) are active in Ladakh. They are committed to put up strong opposition to injustice and tyranny. They are demanding the status of Union Territory for their region.

During the last few decades, extremism and anti-national activities have been in vogue in the State of Jammu & Kashmir. The people of Jammu and Ladakh have been getting treatment as the subjects of the suzerainty of Kashmir for many decades. Voices of opposition, like in Jammu, echoed in Ladakh also. Buddhists are the majority population of Ladakh. It is presumed that Buddhists are not very much concerned with worldly affairs, and they believe in keeping busy with peaceful contemplation and meditation. This wrong perception has been demolished by modern Buddhists. Prominent among them is Shri Tsering Samphel, a Buddhist leader of Ladakh. Shri Samphel, 54, was born in an ordinary rural family. He decided to ensure full development for Ladakh. Though a versatile genius, Shri Samphel did not ignore the social and political problems. He made the best use of Buddhism in organising and activating Buddhists of Ladakh. He opened 'Lamdan' schools at various places. Lam means path, and Dan means light. The schools were supposed to kindle light to show the path. He is president of the Lama Buddhist Association. He is involved actively in many social organisations dedicated for all-round development of Ladakh. He has been fighting the fiscal, social and cultural oppressions perpetrated by State Government for the last about 30 years. He has not yielded, though he was a imprisoned many times. He has generated a very powerful social campaign through the Lama Buddhist Association (LBA). It was a result of the endeavours of LBA that the local branches of National Conference, Indian National Congress and Bharatiya Janta Party dissolved and merged themselves to form a new party called 'Ladakh Union Territory Front' (LUTF), and also obtained support of Muslim organisations of Ladakh. Not only that, the LUTF candidates won the two Legislative Assembly seats of Leh and Nubra, without opposition. A few years back Kushok Bakula, the renowned Buddhist monk of Ladakh, was appointed as Ambassador of India in Mongolia. Because of his talents, devotion to religion and good conduct, Kushok Bakula was regarded as a popular and venerable preceptor by the populace of Mongolia. Very rare would be such instances, where a foreign ambassador is worshipped and offered gifts. That is how the venerable Bakula increased the level of reverence for India in Mongolia.

The Buddhist monks carried from India the lofty ideals of life to many parts of the world. They travelled on foot to countries like China and Japan. They mastered the martial arts like Judo and Karate, and remedies like Acupressure and Acupuncture to safeguard themselves from the obstacles, hindrances, ailments and other stumbling blocks faced by them during their long journeys to foreign countries. These arts and remedies were prevalent in India. The monks carried them from India to China and Japan, from where they came to India back with different names.

It is an irony that after Dr. Ambedkar there has not been proper development of the enormous capabilities of Buddhists, nor the best use of their devotion to *Dhamma* in the process to take Bharat to the pinnacles of glory. The amount of the positive churning of Indian psyche by Dr. Ambedkar, who is believed to be a *Bodhisatva,* has been so great that there may hardly be some people to match him. He had studied Buddhism very profoundly and played a very important role in giving benefit of his studies to common people without any discrimination. It is a matter of great misfortune that some Buddhists are being used by some Christian missionaries.

Noting the trends of the Hindu society taking untouchability as the biggest sin, the Christian missionaries decided to convert the financially- and socially-backward people of Hindu society by pointing out the financial dissimilarities. Their crooked willingness having been exposed now they rake up the issue of poverty for conversion. Their intrigue is conducted under a deep political strategy of trying to change the nationality through conversion. They dream that alien sovereignty can be re-imposed on India by converting the financially- and socially-backward classes to Buddhism, and then, gradually, converting the Buddhists to Christianity. There are reports of Buddhists being used as conduit to convert the financially poor to Christianity. They are being misguided and enticed in various ways to convert to Christianity. It is no less worrying a fact that the intelligentsia and the government are not paying adequate attention to this reality.

As per the Buddha's decree, the Buddhists are supposed to be the '*Atta Deepo*', the source of light themselves. Undoubtedly, Bharat can be taken to the pinnacles of glory if we truly realize Buddha's message of taking refuge in the Buddha, the *Dhamma*, and the Sangh.

□

> *"The whole secret of existence is to have no fear. Never fear what will become of you. Depend on no one. Only the moment you reject all help are you freed."*
>
> **—The Buddha**

28

CHENNAMMA, THE QUEEN OF KITTUR

The way Indian history has been twisted and distorted gives the false impression that India has always been at the receiving end of foreign invaders. Inclusion of such events in history, which could elevate morale of Indians and make them proud of the past of their nation has been avoided meticulously. The real history of Bharat is full of many events that evince that she never drank the pegs of defeat.

For centuries Bharat has been set in struggle modes, but the sycophant historians, flourishing since the times of foreign invasions, even to this date, avoided, deliberately, mention of the valour ballads of bravery and eulogies of the brave Indians in history simply to ensure lasting suppression of their morale. Thus, they tried to see that the morale of Indian people could never be allowed to redeem enough from mental slavery. They have been thinking that the people of Bharat, with paralysed and punctured mentality, would be dominated by their masters and godfathers easily, and then they too could get some *'bakhsheesh'*, tips, from them. Tips included big scholarships, creamy posts, various types of awards and recognitions. As a matter of fact, there has been a long succession of events of barbaric nature confronted and retaliated by Indian society with valour to safeguard its self-esteem and glory at various places, various levels and various degrees. Here is a story of

Rani Chennamma of Kittur (23 Oct, 1778-21 Feb, 1829), the first ever Indian valiant queen to fight against the British. Kittur was ruled by Mallasarja, a seventeen-year-old brave youth and able diplomat. Chennamma was the name of his wife. The Kittur State was spread behind the hills near Belgaum and Pune-Bengaluru highway, and on the areas of Dharwad across the hills. That time the state had 286 villages, 72 hamlets. *Rani* Chennamma was the daughter of Dhullapa Gauda, the head of Kakatigram, which was a part of Sangli State. Her husband passed away at the age of 34 only. *Rani* Chennamma had a decisive moment. She was unwilling to live a life overcome with grief, and die, or a pleasure seeking luxurious life. She gathered courage and decided to tackle all the responsibilities of her husband. Very efficiently she controlled all the administrative machinery of the state. First of all, she increased the efficiency of the intelligence department. She became betenoire of the British. They weaned away three chieftains and a minister from the *Rani*'s fold. She got them back and got them crushed and killed under the elephant's feet. Britishers then attacked Kittur. *Rani* defeated the British because of her sharp intelligence, lustrous vitality, attractive personality, strategic expertise, furiously courageous youthfulness and organising capacity. Prosperity of her state reached pinnacles of glory because of her unique efficiency to take decisions instantaneously, and implement them forthwith. She adopted a boy named Sawai Mallasarja, and nominated him as her successor. The British declared him an illegitimate successor. It was a challenge for the *Rani*. She started preparations to fight the British. British called her for discussion, but the self-respecting *Rani* did not go there. Her spies informed her that the British were going to attack Kittur. So the *Rani* arrested the British political agent, Thackeray, and his two associates as hostage. British army attacked, and a fight began at the main gate of Kittur. The armoured brave Queen Chennamma was leading the army herself. The British army chief Black and Teetan were killed. An all-round cry of agony, distress and panic prevailed in the British army. Their soldiers were dithered and ran away. Balappa, the expert shooter of the queen, shot dead Thackeray. British army was driven away. The queen imprisoned 400 British soldiers. The whole state celebrated the victory, and the *Rani*'s fame spread everywhere. As directed by the British Governor, the British army commanded by colonel Dekal invaded Kittur on 2 December 1829 at midnight. The *Rani* and her army fought valiantly. British army faced furore again. A three-day terrible fight ensued. Paucity of resources continued and the fight could not sustain any longer. The *Rani* was imprisoned. A British doctor injected her with poison, and on 21 February 1829 the *Rani* departed for her heavenly abode, and attained immortality, but her struggle continued.

Rayanna was the name of a gatekeeper of Sangoli. He was in British custody. After ensuring their victory the British released him. He started fighting against the British as soon as he was released. He kept on fighting for two years and occupied Nandgaon, Vidi, Sampagaon and Khanpur. On 28 December 1830, he was arrested and hanged the same day. The unknown brave men like Shankaranna and Nagappa Rajpati crossed swords with British. Sawai Mallasarja, the adopted son of the *Rani*, fought the British again. He was imprisoned, but he ran away from the jail. In 1857, he fought the British again, and the struggle continued.

The struggle is on even today in various forms. The millions of citizens, who are sticking proudly to their supernatural and eternal value systems, have to fight cultural and religious invasions. The sycophants of the foreign powers eying India call them obscurantists and old fashioned. The few so-called advanced people berate and denigrate the supernatural value systems, which is the elixir-seeds of Indian tradition, capable of providing healing atmosphere for entire mankind. The cultural and economic struggle is still on. The wretched and usurping mentality and the strategies of the so-called intellectuals sold in the hands of vested foreign interests will have to be vanquished. There is no alternative. There are millions of Chennammas in our society, particularly in our villages, even today. What is needed is awakening their illustriousness.

□

> *"Change does not roll in on the wheels of inevitability, but comes through continuous struggle. And so we must straighten our backs and work for our freedom. A man can't ride you unless your back is bent."*
>
> **—Martin Luther King, Jr.**

29

SUBRAMANIAN CHANDRASHEKHARA

I am not sure whether it was Shri Ram Krishna Paramhans or Swami Ramtirth who remarked, "Possibly, the Adi Sankaracharya's intelligence was not sharp enough in his childhood, so he took eight years to attain the knowledge of the four *Vedas*." It was the reply to a question, "How could Sankaracharya attain the knowledge of the four *Vedas* by the time he was only eight year old?

Message is clear. One can attain knowledge with birth only. There was a sage called Gulab Rao Maharaj in Vidarbh (Maharashtra) during the preceding century. He was blind since his birth. He was not born in a Brahmin family, and had no background of education and knowledge, still he possessed the knowledge of all scriptures. Not only that, he was acquainted with the philosophy of European philosophers. How could he attain that high degree of knowledge? Answer is clear. It was the wealth of the accumulated *Karmas* of previous births that dawned upon Adi Sankaracharya and the visually impaired Sant Gulab Rao. Now even the Western scientists acknowledge the theory of metempsychosis. After death physical body is cremated, but our ethereal body remains indestructible. Our knowledge and impressions are attached with our ethereal body, which carries knowledge and impressions up to our new births. That explains the marvellous and amazing talents of

Subramanian Chandrashekhara of Chennai. He became a Microsoft professional when he was only nine year old, a certified Microsoft professional. He got admission to engineering college when he was 11, though with some difficulty. It was the liberal attitude of the Chancellor that could enable him get admission to the college. Firstly, mathematics and computer teachers examined him. They acknowledged his noble talents, and recommended him for admission to college to pursue B.E. degree course in computer science. It was not possible according to university rules, so the university syndicate changed the rules. Dr. Balaguruswamy, the university Chancellor said, "The rules should not hinder the progress of such a talented student, that is why we have changed our rules first time. We have full trust that this student will make a new record."

Chandrashekhara had shown his interest in computer science when he was only 6 year old. He topped the list of successful students in the 'National Science Talent Test Examination'. Two universities of America had invited him as an emeritus in the year 2000, but he could not go there, because no visa was given for his parents. We should felicitate him, and simultaneously, the Anna University also, appreciated his talents and gave him admission to B.E. I recall why one of my classmates in M.A., who had passed the examination with good position, could not get appointment as a lecturer simply because his age was less than 18 years.

□

"As the skies appear to a man, so is his mind. Some see only clouds there; some, prodigies and portents; some rarely look up at all; their heads, like the brutes', are directed toward Earth. Some behold there serenity, purity ineffable. The world runs to see the panorama, when there is a panorama in the sky which few go to see."

—Henry David Thoreau

30

DESHONNATI

What is the responsibility of a daily newspaper? Reply to such a question would not be a difficult task. It would be something like this: to provide news, write editorial notes on news, publish readers' ideas and intentions. I have met an owner-cum-editor who goes beyond such expectations.

With whom should go the commitment of a newspaper? With the ideology of the editor or owner? With some party? With the expertise to make money? Or with society? Our society is very large and complex. It has many layers, sections, classes, castes, languages, sects and ideologies. Commitment to such a society means giving space in newspaper, as far as possible, to all of its parts. It would not be possible for any one newspaper, but any news, comment or ideology published in such a newspaper does not become a maxim or the last word of a prophet. It may have other sides also. In my opinion, giving prominence to the other sides is the duty of a newspaper. I have worked as an editor of a Marathi daily. I took it as my duty to publish the views contradictory and reactionary to our editorial intentions. Once I gave the labour column of my newspaper, alternately, to INTUC, BMS, and Lohia Mazdoor Sabha, to be run by their leaders. I regret to say that such an attitude is not there in the big newspapers of Delhi. In recent past, I sent my short comments on an article on terrorism published by a popular English daily.

It was not published, because it did not conform to the views of the editor.

Here I am going to write about a daily newspaper, and its owner-cum-editor, who cares to honour his commitments even beyond the columns of his newspaper. Name of the daily is *Deshonnati*, and the name of the owner-cum-editor is Prakash Pohare.

Deshonnati is published from Akole (Vidarbh) and many other places in Maharashtra. It was started by Congress M.P. Shri Madhusudan Vairale. The paper got a set back after the demise of Shri Vairale. Its circulation came down to only four thousand, then Shri Pohare took care of the paper. As per the ABC certification now the circulation has reached the number ninty-six thousand. There may be many other successful businessmen like Prakash Pohare, but the speciality with him is that he wants to maintain contact with his readers as well as the intelligentsia. That is why he has founded a forum called '*Deshonnati Vichar Manch*'. Four or five speakers have addressed the forum so far. They belong to different ideologies. He had invited me too to address the forum on 19 October 2002. Shri Pohare is neither from R.S.S. nor BJP, but he feels that ideas of various ideologies should be expressed at his forum. His initiative is worth felicitation.

Shri Pohare is trying to turn into reality the name of his paper, Deshonnati, meaning 'Advancement of the country.' Country means, basically, villages, which exist in abundance. So Shri Pohare has started a campaign for the advancement of villages. The campaign is known as '*Gramonnati Abhiyan*'. He has conceived five branches of the campaign. Each branch has seven formulae, known as '*Saptapadi*', the seven-stepped branches. The five branches are as mentioned below:

- "*Krishakonnati*", meaning advancement of farmers. Its *Saptapadi* comprises the following points:

(i) Villages should be free from chemical fertilizers and pesticides, and provided with vermiculture and organic farming.

(ii) Villages should be free from genetically-modified seeds, and provided with indigenously traditional seeds.

(iii) Villages should be free from hybrid breeds of cows and buffaloes, and provided with cow progeny.

(iv) Traditional resources in villages should be preferred to heavy machinery.

(v) Villages should be free from famines, and provided with means to make water available easily.

(vi) Villages should be free from direct marketing of village products. There should be provisions for processing and storage.

(vii) No village should have barren land, and proper vegetation should be grown on such land.

- *Acharonnati Saptapadi.* It means the following seven steps to ensure good conduct and character:

(i) To free villages from animosity and ill-will, and ensure congeniality.

(ii) To free villages from casteism, and ensure prevalence of love for the nation.

(iii) To free villages from convent culture, and provide *Gurukuls*, the traditional seminaries.

(iv) To free villages from foreign aid and provide, as far as possible, indigenous resources.

(v) To free villages from beggary, and see that self-respect prevails.

(vi) To free villages from goondaism and fear, and see that villages have self-defence organisations like '*Prahar*'.

(vii) To free villages from taxes, and encourage them to adopt the traditional practice of *Daana*, donations.

- *Arogyonnati Saptapadi.* It means the following seven-stepped formulae:
  - (i) To free villages from foreign medicines, and encourage Ayurveda and naturopathy.
  - (ii) Free villages from Pepsi, Cola, and tea, and provide them lemon, emblic myrobalan (*Amla*), and provide them cow progeny.
  - (iii) Free villages from alcoholic drinks.
  - (iv) Free villages from cricket, and encourage indigenous sports.
  - (v) Free villages from ignorance and provide gymnasiums, reading rooms and libraries.
  - (vi) Free villages from buffet system of dining, and encourage the *Pangat* system (sitting for common dining).
  - (vii) Free villages from non-vegetarian food, and encourage vegetarianism.
- *Atmonnati Saptapadi*-1. The seven-stepped formulae for self-elevation:
  - (i) Free villages from superstitions, and encourage mutual honour, reverence and trust.
  - (ii) Free villages from mental and psychological deformities, and inculcate cultural values.
  - (iii) Free villages from immoralities, and ensure prevalence of graceful modesty, good conduct and righteousness.
  - (iv) Free villages from ignorance, and ensure development of scientific attitude. Encourage love to read the *Gram Gita.* (It is a popular treatise by Sant Tukdo ji Maharaj of Vidarbh.)
  - (v) Free villages from loose talk and ensure healthy debates.
  - (vi) Free villages from laziness and lackadaisical tendencies, and encourage self-discipline.

(vii) Free villages from inefficiency, and see prevalence of Yoga, and ensure adhering to perseverance.

- *Atmonnati Saptapadi-2*:
  (i) Free villages from indulging in debts, and encourage them to be wealthy.
  (ii) Free villages from small ponds, mosquitoes, garbage and germs. Provide soak pits, and proper sanitation system.
  (iii) Free villages from polluted water and atmospheric pollution. Provide hand pumps, wells and village-tanks.
  (iv) Free villages from externally-imposed leadership, and develop local leadership.
  (v) Free villages from bureaucracy-oriented education. Encourage vocational education.
  (vi) Free villages from rancorous tendencies and litigations. Encourage the *Panchayat* system (village councils).

Shri Pohare did not stop only with the prescription of the theory of the said '*Saptapadi'* for villages. He started the '*Sapta Padis* on ground in five villages.

All that initiative, according to Shri Pohare, stands for progress of the country, *Deshonnati*, which is the name of his newspaper.

□

> *"The one who brings the most satiating results is not the one who is a great genius, but the one who establishes harmonious coordination with the talents of his colleagues is a great genius."*
>
> **—Adage**

31

MAAN BAMALESHWARI BANK FOR WOMEN

Sukvarro is the name of a woman. She is on family way, ready to deliver. Her husband is jobless, parents are poor. She urgently needs rupees five hundred for medical exigencies during delivery and afterwards. From where should she get that money? It was not possible for her neighbours, but everyone wished that she should get necessary help and medical treatment so that she could deliver safely. Their wish was translated into action by some women in the neighborhood. They contributed and collected the sum of rupees five hundred, and gave it to Sukvarro, not as donation, but as a loan. Rate of interest was 2% per month.

Though it was a small incident, yet it caused a bank to appear. It happened in Rajnandagaon, a small town in the state of Chhattisgarh. It is a backward district town, earlier a tehsil, which during British rule was a small State. Women in this district formed twenty self-help groups in nearby regions. They joined hands and formed the 'MAAN BAMALESHWARI BANK'. The bank is run exclusively by women. What is most astonishing is the fact that the bank raised a capital of rupees one crore during a span of one year, and disbursed loan of rupees seventy lakh.

Swati Agrawal, a member of board of directors of the bank says, "We give loan for various needs, right from injections required at the time of delivery to buying old bicycles, ranging from rupees two hundred to rupees ten thousand." 720 self-help groups from the whole Chhattisgarh State are affiliated to this bank. 4500-acre land belonging to the Mahant Digvijay Das Trust is spread across 42 villages of the state. The trust took loan from the bank to develop farming. Both, the bank and the trust were benefitted.

A self-help group affiliated with the bank raised good capital and bought a tractor, which was available to farmers on rentals. Farmers, self-help groups and the bank, all were benefitted. There has been a change in the mentality of women due to the bank. A lady of Somani village says, "Now women of our village have developed a commercial attitude. They have emboldened themselves. They have learned cycling. They use bicycles to fetch drinking water, and fuel wood from jungle, and save both, time and toil." The village women have become courageous to struggle for getting government facilities like electricity and water.

Women empowerment is an issue enshrined in government plans, but it has yet to reach the lower levels. Some women of certain places in Rajnandgaon have empowered themselves through the bank. Women like Rajvanti, Phulsawana, Bimla and Madhulika of the area may not be capable to explain the words 'Women Empowerment' but as the founder members of the 'MAAN BAMALESHWAREE BANK' they do realise the purpose of these words.

□

> *"If you want something said, ask a man; if you want something done, ask a woman."*
>
> **—Margaret Thatcher**

32

FOR SOCIAL HARMONY

"Sewa Bharati" is the name of one of the outfits of the Rashtriya Swayamsevak Sangh (R.S.S.). Its motto is *Sewa*, *Sanskar* and *Samarasata*. *Sewa* means service. The word *Sanskar* does not seem to have got any suitably equivalent word in English language. Broadly, it may mean the collective infusion of sublime qualities like refinement, culture and tradition into the personality of a person. *Samarasata* means harmony and integration.

Here is a description of how Sewa Bharati devotes itself to ensure *Samarasata* in Meerut (U.P.). Its mission has two wings. First, to free the scheduled castes like Valmikis, from inferiority complex by providing them proper education and *Sanskars*, and by elevating their lifestyle from the practices related with sanitation and addiction etc. Second, to liberate the people of the so-called 'upper castes' like Brahmins, Kshatriyas, Vaishyas, etc. from superiority complex, and create an atmosphere that makes them shape brotherly behaviour and affinity with the people of the scheduled and other backward castes.

It is in the light of the initiative to promote samarasata in society that the Sewa Bharati of Meerut Maha Nagar keeps children from communities like Valmiki, etc. with children from the so-called upper castes. Quite often all the children bring food (*roti, paratha*, etc.) from their homes. All the food is deposited at a place, mingled and dumped together. All the children wash their hands properly, sit in lines, and take the mingled food together peacefully after collective chanting of the *bhojan mantra*. No child knows which food stuff came from whose house. Thus, all the children sit together, dine together, study together, and play together. That is how such programmes allay feelings of untouchability, develop affinity, and mitigate all types of complexes of superiority and inferiority. That is what is called samarasata. The years spent in studying together, visiting each other's homes and dining together do not leave any scope to enquire about anyone's caste or tribe. Thus, untouchability is eradicated permanently to a considerable extent.

The children are taken out of city to some park or garden for picnic on holidays. There they play variety of pre-planned games that aim at increasing their ability and capability, and inculcate in them the *Sanskars*. After the games, they sit in a semi-circle, and one by one express themselves through songs, stories, titbits and pleasantries. The games and other activities are conducted by the children themselves. That is how they attain the qualities of hitchless expression, oratory, discipline, effective leadership and maintain and develop their physical and mental fitness. When such activities generate proper development of a child's physique, psyche, mind, sentiments and character, he or she is free from the grips of frustration and dullness. That reflects on every aspect of a child's life. It is better to provide suitable facilities to a child to better lifestyle rather than preaching him or her to become better. The Sewa Bharati centres provide facilities to children without any discrimination, and they develop a sense of competition to score highest marks in examinations. For example, Babita, a student of Jatav community of scheduled caste, studied in Hari Nagar Education Centre of Sewa Bharati, and in July 2001 she scored 78% marks in Junior Engineer examination in 'Instrumentation and Control', held by

Jhansi-based Government Women Polytechnic. She got a job in a reputed factory of NOIDA, U.P. Khushbu, a so-called OBC student of the Hari Nagar Centre, was selected in a competitive examination held by the Uttar Pradesh Polyclinic in 2001, but she chose to prepare for IIT/MNR. Kapil Prakash Jatav passed the competitive entrance examination for Engineering-degree in 2001 from MNR. He is pursuing Electronic Engineering degree course in Lucknow with the cooperation of Sewa Bharati.

Anil Kumar, a Jatav student of Ghantaghar Centre of Sewa Bharati, passed the Junior Engineering examination in Electronics (digital) from Ambedkar Polytechnic, Delhi, in January 2002 with first position. Minal Guglani, a student of Hari Nagar Centre, got admission to Mira Bai Mahila Polytechnic, Delhi, and studied Electronics (Communication). Reena, a student of Jatav Gate Education Centre of Sewa Bharati, was selected in U.P. Polytechnic in 2001. She is studying Electronics in Government Polytechnic at Jhansi. Amit, a Jatav student of the same education centre of Sewa Bharati, was selected in the Polytechnic in 2001. Anil Kumar, a Jatava student of Hari Nagar education centre of Sewa Bharati was selected in MR entrance examination in 2001. He is studying in Gorakhpur Engineering College for degree in Electronics. Amit Kumar, an OBC student of Gautam Nagar Education Centre of Sewa Bharati passed the entrance examination for B.Tech degree from Chaudhari Charan Singh University, Meerut. He is preparing for IIT entrance examination.

As mentioned above, the Maha Nagar Sewa Bharati is concerned not only with the upliftment of the Valmikis and other people of scheduled castes and tribes, it is also concerned with the mentality of people belonging to other castes like Brahmin, Kshatriya, and Vaishya. Here are some instances.

Five girls from Valmiki community, named Anuradha, Shalu, Anu, Supriya and Kanchan were worshipped at the residence of Shri Virendra Kumar Sharma (Rajendra Nagar) during the last year *Navratri Kanya Pujan* programme. Wife and married daughter of Virendra Kumar Sharma washed with their own hands feet of the five girls, and fed them *halwa-pooree* in stainless steel utensils, and bade them farewell, touching their feet, reverentially, with their foreheads, and giving them suitable gifts and cash. Such programmes are convened by Sewa Bharati almost every year.

Since its very beginning Meerut Maha Nagar Sewa Bharati has been running service enterprises like free medical van, a homoeopathic dispensary, *Yogasan Kendra* and tailoring centre for ladies. Such activities generate social consciousness in the comparatively ignored section of the scheduled castes and tribes, and they get good *Sanskars*. This generates *Samarasata*. The workers of Sewa Bharati believe that addictions like smoking, consuming alcoholic drinks, and gambling haunt children because of their bad company during the age groups of 8 to 20 years. They believe that children can be free from such addictions throughout their life if, during these age groups, they are given good thoughts and *Sanskars*. There are more than 1000 beneficiaries including those studying and pass outs. It can be said with conviction that all of them are free from the addictions. These facts are testified in a thesis for Ph.D. degree submitted by Renu, a research scholar from a Valmiki family, in the department of Sociology, C.C.S. University, Meerut.

□

> *"The great secret of true success, of true happiness, is this: the man or woman who asks for no return, the perfectly unselfish person, is the most successful."*
>
> **—Swami Vivekananda**

33

GANESH POOJAN IN A FOREIGN EMBASSY

It may be surprising to know that an idol of Ganesh ji has been installed in the Delhi-based embassy of a European country, and its formal *Arti* is performed daily. Had such an 'excess' been committed in any government office in India the *secular* lobby of Media would have created hullaballoo and commotion, as if Indian Constitution was put at stake. However, the embassy of Ireland kept itself above any such controversy. It seems that the name of Ireland should have been *Aryaland*, i.e. the land of the *Aryas*.

Shri Phillip Macdona, the Ambassador of Ireland in India, installed the Ganesh idol made of black granite, in the compound of his embassy. Present on the occasion was his country's Commerce Minister Shri Mikel Ahema. Obviously, this programme had permission from the Irish Government. It should also be kept in view that the idol was installed not as a showpiece. Daily, it is worshipped, *Arti* performed, and *Prasad* distributed. On the occasion of the installation of the Ganesh idol, Shri Ahema said, "The installation of the Ganesh idol will be auspicious not only for the Irish embassy, it will be a medium of mutual connection of cultures of India and Ireland." He further said, "People of India worship Ganesh ji before starting any programme. We also are going to start a new venture. We are going to boost further our existing commercial relations with India in various ways. We are sure that

Ganesh ji will bless us." Shri Ahema was speaking like a devotee of Ganesh ji. He continued, "Thousands of people come to our embassy every year. They will be glad to see Ganesh ji welcoming them." It happened when Shri Ahema came to India on a government tour.

There were times when Ganesh ji was worshipped all over the world. This fact has been authenticated with evidences by *Bhikkhu* Chamanlalji in his book *Hindu America.* He writes that in America Ganesh ji was worshipped before any baptism. In Europe also Ganesh ji was worshipped before conversion to Christianity. Their deity was Janus, a distorted version of the name of Ganesh ji. It was after the name of Janus that the month of January was started. January is the first month of the European calendar. The description of Janus, as given in the *Encyclopedia Britannia*, resembles that of Ganesh ji to a great extent. The *Encyclopedia* tells, "According to the Roman religious belief 'Janus' is the god of entrance. Bow, in their language, is termed as 'Jaanee'. The word Jaanee was used ceremoniously by them before start of any military march, or any other procession, etc. According to some scholars Janus is originally the deity of start of any work. In common religious programmes 'Janus' is invoked first, before other deities. The sanctity of the word Janus was observed before start of a day, month or year. That is why, January, the name of the first month of a year, indicates pre-eminence of Janus, the deity of start. Many temples were constructed for 'Janus'. The deity has two heads, one with beard, and the other without beard."

□

"We, the Jews, have got a secret weapon in our struggle with Arabs; we have no other place in world."

—Golda Mayar

34

A SOCIAL RENAISSANCE

Very rapid and desirable changes are taking place in Hindu society. Earlier, Southern India was believed to be the stronghold of conservative people where now visible, changes could not have been even imagined about fifty year ago. Now non-Brahmin priests are appointed in temples. Earlier it was a recognised convention that only Brahmins would be entitled to be priests. Contrary to that convention, non-Brahmins are being appointed in temples in Kerala. The matter was dragged to court of Law. The High Court of Kerala upheld the appointments. No doubt, judicial decrees support appropriate social changes, but change cannot take place merely through laws. Laws can only stress upon the change, but it is for the society to implement and live according to them. Society took initiative in Kerala, so non-Brahmins could be appointed as priests. All the Hindu organisations, like the R.S.S. and V.H.P. welcomed the judicial decree, as they were the ones who had initiated the change.

Here is another indication of social change. There was a time when women were not allowed to recite Vedic hymns, although no such ban existed during ancient times. There are references to testify that in the Vedic age there were women with epithets of *Brahmavadini* (the women who spoke the voice of their conscience). The custom of *Upanayana* of girls was also in vogue. Obviously, even girls went to gurus for studies, but this good practice stopped during medieval ages. A convention was decreed that women should not recite Vedic hymns. Nagpur broke that convention. Shri Vidwans Guruji, the Nagpur-based Vedic scholar, taught Vedic hymns to women. He was criticised for it during initial stages, but he did not relent. Now there is a team of women priests in Nagpur. Women priests presided over the religious function convened on the occasion of renovation of the ancestral house of Dr. Keshava Baliram Hedgewar, the founder of the R.S.S., in Nagpur in April 2003. Such miracles were noted in Pune also. There is a public trust called Shrimant Dagadoo Sheth Halwai. It celebrates *Ganeshotsav* with pomp and show, with lots of attractive decorations, so it attracts public extensively. It organised recitation of '*Atharva Sheersha*' by women, fourteen thousand in number. The initiative to teach the '*Atharva Sheersha*' to women was taken in the year 1987. Initially, there were only one hundred women learners. Subsequently, the number rose to fourteen thousand.

It has always been a distinctive trait of Hindu society to welcome change, time to time, in its thought process, customs, conventions, traditions, concepts, conduct, and perceptions. That is why it is ever living and livening. The societies that stop at any point of time cease to exist.

□

> *"Philosophy of life without action is only a dream. Action without philosophy of life is only spending time. It is action with philosophy of life that can change the world."*
>
> **—Jole Arther Barter**

35

'ADARSH-GRAM: SANSKAR-GRAM: SANSKRIT-GRAM'

Kareli is name of a tehsil in district Narsinghpur of Madhya Pradesh. About three kilometre away from Kareli is a village called Mohad, with four thousand population. The distinct feature of this village is that it is a '*Sanskrit village*', imbued with harmony, and that is why it is said to be an ideal village. Notable are the following features of the village:

- Every girl of the village ties Rakhi on wrists of senior citizens.
- Ladies of the village clean not only their houses, but sweep the portions of road in front of their houses. All the roads are un-metalled, so ladies smear the portions of the road with dung.
- 'Om' is written on the doors of all houses.
- Court yard of each house of the village has small flower garden and *Tulsi* plant.
- Shri Ganesh ji occupies seat of honour in the colony of scheduled caste people. On the immersion ceremonies those who shoulder the idol include people from the castes Brahmin and Kshatriya also.
- Nobody is idle in this village. Every child goes to school.

- Every farmer of the village prepares his/her own seeds and fertilizers.
- The cattle wealth in the village is worshipped like deity, and food is cooked on the gas prepared from dung.

No wonder, that this village gets prestige and recognition as an ideal village. It is such unique features of the village Mohad that brought it government award. Not only awarded, Mohad has been decorated with epithets like 'ideal village', and 'the village empowered with good Sanskars'.

The village has some distinct slogans:

- Control and regulate the village-wealth for the village only.
- Control and regulate the village-water for the village only.
- Control and regulate the village-talent for the village only.

Normally, economic progress is believed to be the standard scale to assess development. Mohad has its own standards, and economic progress is only one of the many factors. The real standards are cooperation, harmony, homogeneity, and refined and cultured way of life.

The moment you enter the village you will first have *Darshan* of Hanuman temple. The Ramayana couplet "*Pravisi Nagar keejai sab kaja, Hriday rakhi kosal pur raja*", written on the temple, will welcome you. Go ahead, and you will see well-cleaned and dung-smeared-path ways with both sides having shadowy trees of *Peepal*, *Ashok, Neem*, and *Imli*.

Who made Mohad such a beautiful and fascinating

village? No doubt, it was the collective will and energy of the whole village, which worked to make it as it is, but the credit to inspire the people of the village goes to Thakur Surendra Singh Chauhan. He was a teacher, resigned his job and settled in the village. He is a dedicated *Swayamsevak* of the R.S.S. Earlier he was the *Karyavah* (General Secretary) of R.S.S.-*Koshal Prant*. For the last three years, he has been a member of the National Executive Council of R.S.S., and works as *Akhil Bharatiya Sah Sewa Pramukh*. The subject of *Gram Vikas* (village development) also comes under the jurisdiction of the *Sah Sewa Pramukh*. As an all India official of the *Gram Vikas* project, Shri Surendra Singh has to tour the whole country regularly as planned by the R.S.S. Villagers call him Bhaiya ji. Meet him, and speak to him in any language, Shri Surendra Singh will reply in Sanskrit only. All the letters he receives he replies in Sanskrit only. He was not a Sanskrit teacher. As far as I know he taught English, but after coming into contact with Shri Cha Mu Krishna Shastri of the Sanskrit Bharati he also became a Sanskrit lover. Shri Krishna Shastri talks in Sanskrit only. In his small village, Shri Surendra Singh Chauhan convened a camp of '*Sanskrit Sambhashan Kendra*', the Centre of Discourse in Sanskrit. He motivated the village students to attend the camp, and the whole village embraced Sanskrit through education and practice in the camp. In this village, Sanskrit is not the language of Gods. All villagers, even children, irrespective of the dividing factors like caste, etc. speak in Sanskrit. The villagers were almost illiterate about fifteen years ago. Today there are five schools in the village. Now more than 45% of the villagers are literate.

Needless to say that there runs a good R.S.S. *Shakha* in the village. Nobody can hold up our dear *Bharat* from becoming a great nation if all villages of the country emulate village Mohad.

□

"Biggest is the Earth. Why Earth? It is situated on the head of Sesh, so Sesh is the biggest. How Sesh is the biggest? Sesh is lying clung to Shankar ji's neck, so Shankar ji is the biggest. Oh! How Shankar ji is the biggest? He moves around sitting on the back of Nandi, so Nandi is the biggest. Oh! How Nandi is the biggest? He rests on Kailash, so Kailash is the biggest. Oh! How Kailash is the biggest? It was uprooted by Ravan three times, so Ravan is the biggest. Oh! How can Ravan be the biggest? He was clung to the cradle of Kumar Angad at the residence of Bali, so Bali is the biggest. Oh! How can Bali be the biggest? He was knocked down by only one arrow of Ram ji, so Ram ji is the biggest. Oh! How can Ram ji be the biggest? He prostrates on the feet of saints. Therefore, Saints are the biggest."

—Adage

36

WANT TO MEET THE M.L.A.? GO TO HOSPITAL

A man is sitting at a bench in front of the 'Out Door Patients' department of a big hospital of the city. Dressed in white he is surrounded by crowd of patients. He is busy in arranging medicines, blood and ambulance for the patients. Beside him are three almirahs that store medicines. He directs a man standing nearby and the latter very promptly writes something in a register. This white-dressed gentleman is not a doctor, nor a *Swayamsevak*. He is a Member of Legislative Assembly (MLA) from Junagarh, Gujarat, named Mahendra Mashru, preparing this time to contest on BJP ticket. He is a unique MLA. He does not take the salary an MLA is entitled to draw, nor does he use any facility available to an MLA. In the Legislative Assembly, he never supports any proposal or resolution that recommends increment in the facilities and perquisites for MLAs. A few years back he created a situation of moral crisis for other MLAs when he opposed such a resolution very strongly. He has been winning elections for the last two terms as an independent candidate from Junagarh. This time BJP has nominated him as its MLA candidate. That will benefit BJP more than himself.

Mashru is a bachelor. He lives in Junagarh with his brothers. For his living, he serves in a local cooperative bank. He spends only a part of his salary on himself, and the rest he spends in activities related with public welfare. He dines only once a day, and has nothing to do with addictions like cigarette, *bidi* or tobacco.

Normally, Mashru can be contacted daily from morning to noon at the same very bench of the hospital, but he reaches first to any place of crisis. After the 1995 elections, when all the candidates and their supporters were present vigilantly at the ballot counting centre in the district collector's office, Mashru Saheb was shouldering the dead body of an unknown person to crematorium. Even during these elections, Mashru was not visible anywhere, unlike other candidates canvassing vociferously in streets with drums and tymbals. A search by some journalists revealed that Mashru was busy in serving a wounded cattle in a corner of the city. He told them, "This animal's leg is badly wounded. How can I leave it in this condition and go for canvassing?" His priorities are excellent, but the problem is that his saintly nature causes a lot of deep inferiority complex in other MLAs. Many philanthropic institutions came forward to aid Mashru with ambulances, and medicines worth lakhs of rupees that are stored in the almirahs kept in a corner of the hospital. Very rarely does a patient take medicines from the medical store of the hospital.

There cannot be any problem to any patient as long as Mashru is around.

□

> *"If my mind can imagine a thing, and my heart can believe in it, I will certainly achieve it."*
>
> —**Adage**

37

HOSPITAL IN SIACHEN

Siachen glacier is situated at a height of 22,000 feet from the sea level. Standing there you will find snow and snow, every side up to any place you can view. Hailstorms are common there. Though the whole landscape is unique and beautiful, the climate is dangerous. During the deep darkness at nights, temperature falls down upto 50 degrees below zero. The bone-chilling icy winds, and lack of oxygen, are quite challenging. It is in such adverse circumstances that our brave soldiers are posted there to defend the Motherland.

Lieutenant General Arjun Rai, the General Officer Commanding of 14th Corps of Ladakh, tells about the Army post at Siachen, "It is such an Army post where our soldiers attain martyrdom, more from climate than enemy bullets."

If not treated timely, the climate hit soldiers hardly survive. It is for such treatment of the soldiers that a hospital has been established at Siachen. Furnished with all modern facilities, the hospital is situated at a place called Hoondar. It was inaugurated on November 18, 2001 by the then Defence Minister Shri George Fernandes. The 45-bed hospital has proved to be a boon not only for the soldiers, but also for the residents of Nubra valley.

The story of the construction of this hospital is very interesting. It starts from the time of Kargil War. Various institutions, newspaper groups, and industrialists had raised funds for the welfare of soldiers at the time of Kargil War. Various organisations and institutions contacted the masses and requested them to cooperate. Inspired by the feelings of patriotism, the masses contributed some portion of their income for the cause. The Kolhapur (Maharashtra)-based Maratha daily newspaper named '*Pudhari* '(meaning the one who leads) raised a capital of rupees two crore five lakh. How this capital was raised is narrated by Shri Pratap Singh Jadhav, the editor of *Pudhari,* "Thousands of persons came forward to aid. Ordinary peasants, labourers, working women, freedom fighters, all contributed. Not only that, even children contributed out of their birthday-party funds, and the sum total of the contribution was rupees two crore five lakh." Shri Jadhav invited the Defence Minister Shri Fernandes to hand him over this money for the Central Army Welfare Fund. While inaugurating the hospital, Shri Fernandes recalled the occasion and said, "When I went to receive the contributed money I was remembering the brave soldiers posted at Siachen. For a long time I was feeling the need of a modern hospital at Siachen, but the Defence Ministry could not allot the required funds. When Shri Jadhav handed over to me a bank draft for rupees two crore five lakh I decided to use the money in construction of a hospital at Siachen. Today that resolve has taken shape. The contribution of General Arjuna Rai has been immense. The completion period, as told at the planning stage in the Ministry, was to be three years, because of the fact that the construction work could be carried out only for about 3 to 4 months of a year, with remaining months witnessing frozen ice. Labourers too are not available. Though it was a tough mission, General Rai resolved and declared that it would be completed within five months only. Indeed, General Rai fulfilled his challenging resolve quite successfully within the given period." The *Bhoomi Poojan* ceremony was performed on 4 July 2001, and the hospital was inaugurated on 19 November 2001. It is truly a glorious record.

How needed was the hospital at Siachen was evidenced by the fact that many soldiers and common citizens of the locality were admitted in the hospital for treatment even before it was inaugurated formally. Major Rajiva Singhal, the Surgical Specialist of the hospital gave a brief account of the facilities available in the hospital, "The 45-bed hospital is meant mainly for the soldiers posted at Siachen, but it has got a family ward also, for treatment of the local population. It has paediatrics and maternity wings also. It is affiliated with MAC, the Medical Aid Complex. Since it is furnished with central heating mechanism, it has special facilities to treat ailments caused at places of high altitudes and icy regions. It has got a special cell to condition the normal air pressure, which remains very low outside."

The local population is very happy with this hospital. Three year old Ali Rahmat of Partapura underwent a surgery here. His father says that Rahmat had a fracture in his left hand-bone, which has been treated through surgery. Extra precautions have to be observed while administering anaesthesia. Great care has to be taken to maintain the normal activities of heart and lungs during the stage of unconsciousness, all that depends on oxygen.

Indeed, Siachen is a miracle, which highlights the duty and resolve of our Army.

□

> *"Leadership has to be built on the strong foundation of life-values. If the life-philosophy directs life, the life-values determine dignity and decorum."*
>
> **—Azim Premji**

38

FRIKSHON LINGDOH

Meghalaya comprises mainly of three tribes, Garo, Jayantiya, and Khasi. More than 90% of the Garo and Jayantiya tribes have converted to Christianity. About 50% of Khasis have also converted to Christianity, but for the last about two decades there has been a renaissance among Khasis about their religion, traditions, customs and identity. Anderson Mavari was the pioneer of this new revolution. It is in that tradition of change that the name of Frikshon Lingdoh is also distinct and in forefront.

On 31 January 2002, Shri Lingdoh was accorded a very hearty and emotional honour by Vivekanand Kendra Institute of Culture (VKIC). The VKIC started honouring distinguished persons who contributed to the renaissance in the last four years. Shri Lingdoh is the fourth recipient of the honour. The earlier three honoured persons were Dr. Pradip Chaliha of Assam, Tadak Gara of Arunachal Pradesh, and Yose Chaya of Nagaland.

Shri Lingdoh started his address with these words, "Brothers and sisters who have come here from the hilly and plain areas of Bharat Mata." He said further, "Initially I could not understand why a common man like me living in a small village of a corner of the country has been selected for this prestigious award. Later I came to know that the Vivekananda Kendra is committed to preserving the cultural traditions and beliefs of the tribes, so I gave my willingness to accept the award. The prime aim of my life is to preserve and protect the most ancient culture and the traditional beliefs given to us by God. I have always craved that our people should be ever conscious of that. In the year 1960, I had accepted the post of Lingdoh of Himarivarim. Since then I have been trying to strengthen the religious order of the original Khasis. It was with the aim of reinforcing our religion and belief system that I discussed the issue with the leaders of Seng Khasi tribe and founded the organisation. We tried to hold meetings of our youth of rural and urban areas to make them conscious of our roots. The first convention of the Seng Khasi youth was held in village Nang Krem. I was secretary of that convention. My dear brothers and sisters, we all are offspring of Bharat Mata. It is from this pious soil that our religion and belief emerged. We may have some differences, but we believe that our God is one and the same. As rivers originate from different places, but all of them run to end in ocean, so all of our religions and faiths lead us up to the same supreme creator. I am proud of my faith, my culture and traditions. I understand that the purpose of giving me the award is boosting my morale to do even more public service."

In his address, Shri Lingdoh emphasised that the culture and traditions of Khasis of Meghalaya are unique, but there is great similarity between them and those of the other states of India. It is this similarity, which ensures unity amongst us. A new zeal has been generated in Meghalaya by that convention, and the efforts of the Christian missionaries to destroy faith and traditions of the tribes, and spread Christianity have been halted. Not only that, the Khasis who had converted to Christianity are returning home to their own faith. Such desired changes are transforming the image of Meghalaya.

□

"Endurance in adversities, forgiveness in rise, impressive eloquence in society of learned, valour in battle, attentiveness in learning and spreading reputation, and indulgence in knowledge; these are the natural traits of gentlemen."

—Adage

39

WELCOME DAWN OF DESIRABLE CHANGE

Most of the people of district Jhabua in Madhya Pradesh are forest dwellers. Far from having modern traits, it is almost a forest populace, which was earlier believed to be a sanctuary of crimes and criminal gangs. The village Machhaliyaghat was supposed to be the ring leader of persons with criminal instincts. The rare visit of any government official to this village entailed a fleet of security vehicles around the vehicle of the official. What to say about common people! All means of communications stopped as soon as dusk fell.

Now the atmosphere of Machhaliyaghat and the nearby areas has changed. It appears that the deep darkness of night has vanished and dawn appeared.

This magical awakening was caused by the Hindu Renaissance. Shri H.V., Seshadri ji, the *Sah Sar Karyavah* of R.S.S., visited this area. He noted the changes, and described them: "I visited the same very district in the month of November. We reached there via Machhaliyaghat. On the way, we saw many vehicles, buses, etc. carrying passengers. It was quite a normal scene, and a welcome change. It reminded me of the huge difference between earth and sky. I was accompanied by some prominent workers of the Sangh and Vanvasi Kalyan Ashram. I was told that the change had taken place during the last couple of years. It was natural not to disbelieve what they said. I took some time to believe in that.

Machhaliyaghat : A Symbol

"We went to a habitation called Junapani. It is adjacent to Machhaliyaghat. There, inside the hut of Shri Raja Ram Katara, we sat near the hearth and took hot *rotis* of maize flour baked by the matriarch of the household. While talking to the host family members, I got a glimpse of the auspicious changes. Shanti is the name of a girl of this family. She has appeared in 12th class examination, and teaches in a school nearby Ratlam district, and, is simultaneously, preparing for further studies. Once an old teacher of that school asked Shanti which place she belonged to, and what were her educational qualifications. On coming to know that she was from Machhaliyaghat the teacher remarked ridiculously, "You belong to the loin clad Bheel tribe?" Shanti retorted in a shrill tone, "Do you find any difference between you and me? You are a human being, so are we, but you preserve an inferiority complex for me. You feel that you are better than us. We do not preserve that egoism in our mind. We believe in equality among all of us." We can imagine the state of mind of the teacher on hearing Shanti's remarks. He left the place quietly. This incident is just like a ray of a fine morning Sun in the life of the forest dwellers of Machhaliyaghat and nearby areas.

"Megh Nagar, a tehsil centre of district Jhabua, looks like a city. I had a detailed discussion with the workers of R.S.S., Sewa Bharati and the Vanvasi Kalyan Ashram etc. of that area. It was nice to know that the changes in lifestyle of the forest dwellers were quite pervasive, and eventually, there were many auspicious results. Barely two years earlier it was beyond imagination for city dwellers to step into any village of the *Vanvasis* (forest dwellers) after 6 p.m., but now the circumstances have changed drastically. Now we can move out of Megh Nagar, and come back even during midnight by motor bikes." They gave us some wonderful information in that context, "Police records, in the language of police, show that there were '100% murders' during last three years in village Sokha of tehsil Alirajpur in Jhabua district. In the year 2001, the number came down to 50%, and in the year 2002 there was no murder in the area of Alirajpur police station as per the police records, which mention that the number of incidents pertaining to plunder, destruction and dacoity was zero in the year 2002. Earlier it was common that even small provocations caused a chain of murders, stopping buses on road, deboarding the passengers belonging to opposition villages forcibly, and killing them. Now all such practices have stopped.

Change in the Life of the Bhagats

"There have been some more vital changes in the last couple of years, which are visible in the forest-dwelling area. A community called Bhagat lives in the area. People of this community do not take alcoholic drinks and non-vegetarian food. As per their belief they live pure, pious, and virtuous life. That makes them feel that they are superior to others. Their complex behaviour continued for ages, but now there has been a remarkable change. We went to a small village called Moi in tehsil Petalavada. The tehsil *Sanghchalak* Shri Nathulal ji Damra is a Bhagat. He has mixed up with the wave of renaissance among the forest dwellers. Some prominent villagers of nearby areas congregated on a night in the village to hold a meeting. Shri Nathulal ji Damra addressed the meeting, "As a Bhagat I too was a victim of that mentality of superiority, but now I am fully convinced that we all are Hindus. If we do not get organised as Hindus, and cut ourselves off from the mainstream, nobody can save us from the clutches of missionaries. Therefore, we must free ourselves from the complex that we, as Bhagats, are superior to other brothers and sisters of the Vanvasi Kshetra (area of the forest dwellers). We must treat them on equal footing. Then only we can remain safe. It would be impossible to live as Bhagats if other religions hunt us.

"Such an instance came to notice in another village called Bada Sameliya in district Jhabua. A renowned saint known as Kanu Maharaj lives in that village. He is also a Bhagat. He expressed the change that he had embraced in a very emotional and poetic manner, "Earlier I was flowing in a small drain of the Bhagats, now I have gained homogeneity with the great flow of Ganga ji of Hindu society."

Conversion and Home-coming

Conversion is a problem, which has been crucially related with survival of Hindu *Dharma* and Hindu society. It has been a common presumption that district Jhabua has for ever been a place well nurtured to welcome Christianity. The Pope had declared this district as an independent communal, Christian state, known in roman language as '*diocese*'. Maximum number of nuns and priests or '*padres*' were posted there to propagate Christianity. Huge amount of funds were allotted to this '*state*' for that purpose. As per the media reports earlier, it appeared that the whole district was an established sovereignty of Christians. Now, with the gradual renaissance of Hindutva that sovereignty is diminishing."

Some Instances

Years ago, in the initial stages, our *Karyakartas* had to approach the local populace, and convince them to join our activities. The Christian effect often created stiff opposition. Now the situation has changed. Now the local people invite our *Karyakartas*. Out of the 3500 families settled there, 63 Christian gentlemen, ladies and children returned to their *Matri Dharma* in a first home-coming. There was opposition earlier from many other villages, but now they themselves invite our *Karyakartas*. As a result of the overwhelming prevalence of Hindutva in the whole region, only four out of the thirty two villages are now in touch with Christians.

There is a church in Amkhut division near Alirajpura tehsil, which is as old as Christianity in the area, 106 year old. More than 50% of the nearby population is Christian. There was a programme of *Bharart Mata Pujan* in that locality. At least five old men present in the programme had tears in their eyes. They said, "See how unlucky we are. Our boys have converted to Christianity. They do not treat us as father. They call a Christian padre as father. Swami Asimanand ji Maharaj visited that place, and led a procession of Hindus. There was a meeting after the procession.One hundred and thirty-five Christian men, women and children standing nearby were also invited to attend the meeting, and they attended it. They heard Maharaj ji, and decided to come back to their original fold of Hindutva. They took a holy bath and became Hindus formally.

Conversion to Christianity has been banned totally in Alirajpura and Bhabhra tehsils of district Jhabua. The process of home-coming is continuing gradually.

Start of Self-Help

A Self-Help Centre has been opened in Kukshi tehsil of district Dhar. Last year 16 of our *Vanvasi Bandhus* from that place started a grocery shop. A loan of ₹ 19,000/-, taken to raise initial capital for the shop, has been returned within a year, and there was saving of ₹ 1200/- in a month. Grocery worth ₹ 25,000/- is stored. Some Pune-based businessmen also gave them the grocery on loan at cheap rate of interest, which was paid back timely. The families, which subscribe ₹ 50/- per month to the Self-Help Centre can purchase grocery on very cheap rates. After a fixed time schedule, the subscribers get back their invested money with a part of profit. Members of 70 families get the opportunity to work for the shop. Inspired by this popular initiative seven nearby villages have also started grocery shops.

It was natural for the then Congress Government of Madhya Pradesh to get worried due to the Hindu renaissance in the area of the forest dwellers. When government officials reach them with development plans to help them economically they retort plainly, "We shall develop ourselves with our own organised efforts."

□

"The best leader is not the one who is praised by people, gets hailing applauds and obedience from public. The best leader is the one who is not well known, who keeps quiet after attaining goal, while others keep claiming, "We have attained our goal."

—Adage

40

'SHEGAON' AN OCEAN OF BLISS

What activities should be carried out by a religious institute? It may sound ignorance, and attract comments like "Oh! Religious institutes should do religious works like *Bhajans* (devotional hymns), *Kirtans* (religious stories accompanied by music), *Pooja* (worship), *Arati* (ceremonial adoration with kindled lamps), *Prasad* (gift from a deity) and *Pravachans* (sermons) etc." However, such limits are not acceptable to the Shri Gajanan Maharaj Institute of Shegaon. There is much more to be done apart from *Bhajan-Kirtan*, etc. We will have to accept that all activities that contribute to the welfare of the society come within the ambit of *Dharma,* if we understand the meaning of the word *Dharma.* Religion is too poor a translation and substitute of *Dharma* to unfold and explain the pervasive purport of *Dharma. Dharma* pervades life. It has to do with both, worldly life and the life hereafter. In our Hindu philosophy, *Dharma* is not only for other worldly wealth? That is why the *Mahabharat* says, "*Dharanad Dharma Ityahuh, Dharmo Dharayti Prajah.*" It means that *Dharma* upholds, sustains, protects and preserves those who bear it. It is called *Dharma*, the expression that comprises merit, virtue, righteousness, dutifulness, etc. It pervades not only mankind, but all life. There is an institute, which comprehends and bears this grand attitude. It is known as Gajanan Maharaj Sansthan, Shegaon. Shegaon is the name of a place situated near Akole, about 350 kms from Nagpur on western side. Gajanan Maharaj was an *Avadhoota* or an *Avaliya*, an ascetic, who had renounced all worldly attachments and connections. Though the view that he was Nana Saheb Peshawa, the freedom fighter of the war of Independence of 1857 has not been acknowledged in popular imagination, it is sure that the *Avadhoot* appeared in Shegaon on 23 February 1878, and completed his life-journey in Shegaon only on 8 September 1910. Nobody knows how old the *Avadhoota* was when he appeared in Shegaon, and nobody knows what was his age when he passed away.

The number of followers of Shri Gajanan Maharaj, who believe in his spiritual supremacy, has been increasing regularly. The readers and interpreters of literature about the sage is spread all over Maharashtra. It is not only the adults and the old, who read his literature, young boys and girls also read it with great reverence. It is believed that the books fulfil all wishes of the devotees.

This institute is distinct from others of its kind because its mission is not only academics, but, is service-oriented also. It may be surprising to know that the institute runs even an Engineering College, which is affiliated to Amaravati University, and recognized by the A.I.C.T.E. of Delhi. Even this Engineering College holds programmes for refinement of students' personality. Credit for that goes to the Principal, Dr. Vakde. Prayer and Saraswati *Vandana* are recited in every class in the very beginning of daily schedule. Students from all sects and communities sing together. Though it is an Engineering College, it runs classes in Sanskrit discourse also. Apart from that the institute runs a residential school for mentally retarded, the *Divyangs*, with a hostel to accommodate

82 students, with free food and lodge. A hermitage for primitive people is also run by the institute. It runs an institute to impart education in *Varakari Kirtan*, which is a distinct feature of Maharashtra. In northern India, *Kirtan* means only congregational singing of devotional songs in commemoration of a deity. In Maharashtra, *Kirtan* means musical sermon. There are two streams of *Kirtan* in Maharashtra. One is known as *Naradiya* and the other as *Varakari*. In *Naradiya Kirtan*, the main singer/sermoniser is accompanied with two others, one playing harmonium, and the other tabla, a set of two pieces of drums. The main singer/sermoniser, called '*Kirtan Kara*', first of all presents some philosophical doctrine, which is known as *Brahmaniroopan*, elucidation of the eternal spirit. It is followed by detailed explanation through anecdotes and stories. This part is known as *Kathaniroopana*, the elucidation of katha, the story narration. The *Katha* part is not there in *Varakari* school of *Kirtan*. In this stream, sermons are delivered on any *vachan* (utterance) of a saint. That *vachan* is sung in rhythmic tunes. At least eight to ten music players stand behind the main *Kirtankar*. One of them plays a veena (lute or harp). Both of these streams of *Kirtan* are practised popularly even today for educating the masses.

Among the service projects of the institute are Allopathic, Homoeopathic, and Ayurvedic dispensaries. There are three mobile clinics and one pathological laboratory. There is provision for Naturopathy also.

On 16 January 2003, the then Vice-President of India, Shri Bhairon Singh Shekhawat, inaugurated a novel project of the institute called Anand Sagar (Ocean of Bliss) in Shegaon. The guiding spirit behind this beautiful 350-crore project is 63-year-old Shiv Shankar Patil. It is a replica of the famous Vivekanand Rock Memorial of Kanyakumari. Patil is the present president of the institute. Though a heart patient, he is a uniquely talented organiser. Looking at his disciplined zeal and devotion, nobody can imagine that he is a heart patient. He has been serving Gajanan Maharaj Institute for the last 42 years. Though not highly educated formally, his dedication and devotion to duty make him distinct. Physically frail he lives a simple life, but his committed devotedness makes him very strong. He does not accept even a single favour, in cash or kind, from the Institute he serves, directs and supervises. He renders absolutely free services to the Institute.

It was the result of three years devoted service of the extremely sweet and soft spoken, but formidably determined, Shiv Shankar Patil that Anand Sagar came into being. It is really an Ocean of Bliss. The moment you see the entry gate of Anand Sagar, you feel infatuated. In front of the Jaipur red stone gate is a parking space to park five hundred cars, and nearby, a rest house for drivers.

The moment you enter the gate you will see a statue of Yogiraj Sant Gajanan Maharaj, and statues of eighteen prominent saints of different communities. The scene evokes your desire to go ahead and see more. You will find a vast space decorated with varieties of trees, creepers, multi-coloured flowers, vast green lawns, structures for shelter, and beyond that a vast lake. Kanyakumari has got natural sea. Here is a man-made lake having white boats that gives the impression of swimming white herons. The lake contains islands, which are covered with greenery. Rowing over the waters provides a good entertainment. The main island has got a hut for meditation. There are hanging bridges to connect the islands with each other. There is a meeting-pavilion for public programmes, and also a beautiful aquarium. There are many apparatuses for entertainment of children, like a 3-km long rail with a train, and innumerable electronic toys. There is a food village, the *Anna Gram*, where one can have different types of eateries and dishes, all of them, invariably, vegetarian.

The whole campus is absolutely neat and clean. Some works are still in progress; but there is no sign of any untoward happening or arbitrary conduct. The lesson of devotion to duty silently seems to have been taken from the conduct of Shiva Shankar ji. As the scented *Shrikhand* (a sweet) is made with a mixture of curd and saffron, so seems to be the addition of religious devotion with every activity of the Institute. Even an ordinary labourer does not take salary for one day in a week. The stone cutter who chisels stone for sculpting idols says, "I am contributing in the temple construction just as the squirrel contributed in making path on sea for Ram." Needless to say anything about the devotional contribution of other senior workers after knowing the feelings of labourers and skilled workers. Five hundred labourers have been working there daily for the last three years, but there is no office. Six supervisors and eighteen contractors have been working relentlessly. As the experts say, the project, which would have taken ten years for completion in normal circumstances, has been completed in three years.

On an average, an amount of ₹ 3 lakh is offered daily. Thus, the annual income is ₹ 11 crore. The Institute gets subscriptions in the form of donations, etc. to the tune of ₹ 8 to 10 crores annually. The Institute has gained the trust of the public that all that money will be invested only in good work. It is on the basis of that trust and belief that this elegant tourist place has come up.

The whole project covers an expanse of 350 acres of land. The first phase has been completed on 120 acre. The second and third phases will cover the projects related to Amusement Park, Water Park, Peace Garden (Shanti Van), Musical Fountain, Planetarium, Bhool Bhulaiya (labyrinth), and Light and Sound system on the life and activities of Shri Gajanan Maharaj. Shri Shiv Shankar ji has full trust that the projects would be accomplished with the inspiration of Swami Vivekanand ji and blessings of Gajanan Maharaj.

□

> *"The best way to find yourself is to lose yourself in the service of others."*
>
> **—Mahatma Gandhi**

41

'DHAGEVADI' A PILGRIMAGE OF LABOUR

Dhagevadi is name of a small village. '*Dhag*' in Marathi language means cloud. Located at very high altitude it seems to be touching clouds, so it is named as 'Dhagevadi'. It is situated in tehsil Akole, district Ahmadnagar, Maharashtra. There is no way to reach the village except footpath. The height is so much that one pants heavily while reaching there even empty handed. The village has only 55 families, all of them forest dwellers, belonging to the tribe called 'Mahadevkoli' in Maharashtra. *Koli* in Marathi means fisherman. Total population of the village is about 300. It has 371 hectare land, out of which cultivable is only 184 hectare. On average, normally, annual rainfall is 50 cm, but all of the rain water, earlier, flowed down due to high altitude of the location. Still the villagers produced some millet, paddy and ground nut in the mostly unirrigated land, and as soon as the rainy season was over they migrated to other places for jobs, and returned before rainy season. Almost for half a year, the entire working male population used to be out of the village, rendering it idle. A few children went to cities for further studies after completing primary education in the village.

Bhaskar Pardhi was one of the students who passed 4th class and went to tehsil town for further education.

He got admission into a hostel run by the Vanvasi Kalyan Ashram. He passed 10th class while living in that hostel. What to do next was the question he faced for some time, and then he decided to do something for his village. He had some friends in the village, who also decided to do something for the village, but they did not know what to do. In the meantime, Bhaskar came to know about a 40-day camp to be run by 'Suyash Charitable Trust' near Pune. The camp had a programme about imparting training in how to grow vegetables, foster goats, and how to avail benefits of government schemes. Bhaskar attended that camp, and the training of 40 days brought him inspiration and new zeal. He decided to experiment his newly, gained knowledge himself first in his small village, which was free from politics, and therefore, free from mutual wrangles and disputes. There was complete unity in the village.

Initially, he, along with three farmers of his village, decided to cultivate tomatoes. The Suyash Charitable Trust provided them good seeds. All the technical knowhow about how to sow, type of manure to be used, when and how much, how and when to spray insecticides, when and how much to irrigate, when to pluck and market the crop, was provided by the Trust. It deputed its workers to visit the village almost every week. This experiment of Bhaskar and his fellow friends was quite successful. The villagers were encouraged, so they decided to raise a project for holistic development of their village. Fifteen farmers gave their 22-acre barren land for the project. They planned to plant trees, in the first year in order to check the village from strong gusts of wind. All around the land they planted five hundred eucalyptus trees, and on the remaining land were planted one thousand five hundred trees of different categories. The first summer endangered the plants. Two donkeys were employed to fetch water in plastic drums tied on their backs, from two km down, to irrigate the plants. About 90% plants survived. The hill appeared green. This project, called *Haritgarh*, sustained with glory.

The tomato production also increased. Now the problem was how to carry the produce down to the market. There was no way, so the villagers carved out a path through *Shramdan*, the voluntary labour, and took some other good decisions as mentioned below:

- All the village land will be cultivated.
- The village will be free from intoxicants.
- Once a week every villager will do the *Shramdan,* without any payment.
- Water will be checked for the village.
- Restrain villagers from going out of the village for employment.

With these decisions, the villagers devoted themselves in self-help, and with their own labour built four small dams. Then came help from government also. It built six dams to check water drain down. There was a grant for three bore wells yearly.

Tomato production increased with availability of water. 20-25-acre land produced tomato. Another problem arose. Rate of tomato fell down with the growth in its yield. The villagers consulted the workers of Suyash, and came into existence the institution called "Ambe Mata Abhinav Tomato Sauce Utpadak Sanstha", the "Ambe Mata Novel Tomato Sauce Producers Cooperative Institute." Production of tomato sauce started. Now Dhagevadi sent to market tomato sauce bottles, not tomatoes. The flow of income made villagers forward looking. A '*Balvadi*' (school for children), known as 'Shishu Mandir', started. 25-30 cows were purchased and dairy business also started. An assembly pavilion was erected near the temple, where they observed *Hari Nam Saptah* (Week for congregational recitation of hymns) each year. A Datta temple was also built. Now every *Ekadashi* people recite *Bhajans.* Two students from Dhagevadi passed 12th class examination with 1st position.

Three-wheeler vehicles started coming to Dhagevadi, but they charged too much, so the villagers purchased a jeep and a three-wheeler vehicle. Now they have got their own means of transportation.

On 29 November 2002, the initiative was inaugurated formally. Shri Jagdev Ram Oraon, the president of the Akhil Bharatiya Vanvasi Kalyan Ashram, and Shri Bindu Madhav Joshi, the founder of the Akhil Bharatiya Grahak Panchayat came to Dhagevadi for the inauguration. Shri Bindu Madhav Joshi was the chief speaker. He said, "I do not felicitate you, I adore you. May be, it took 55 years, but you have told the correct meaning of Independence and self-reliance to people as well as the government. With your self-respect and your hard work you have transformed the rough and dry hill into a sort of lush green bower of Indra Dev. You have presented a great ideal of development. Your village, Dhagevadi, has indeed become a sacred place of pilgrimage of labour. Bravo to you."

□

> *"The best way to not feel hopeless is to get up and do some thing. Don't wait for good things to happen to you. If you go out and make some good things happen, you will fill the world with hope, you will fill yourself with hope."*
>
> **—Barack Obama**

42

CHAIT RAM OF *BARIPADA*

His name is Chait Ram Pawar. It should have been Chaitanya Ram, because it fits into his deeds. He is M.Com, but he never tried to get a salaried job. As soon as he completed his education, he came back to his village called Baripada, situated in district Nandurbar, on the border of Maharashtra and Gujarat. The whole district of Nandurbar is filled with forests. Baripada is also amidst forests. Earlier one had to walk on foot for at least five km to reach the village. Even a jeep could not reach there. Now things have changed. Credit for the change goes to Chait Ram.

There is a town called Varsa near Baripada. A health centre is run in the town by Vanvasi Kalyan Ashram. Dr. Anand Pathak works in that centre. More than a decade ago, Dr. Pathak went to the village for the first time, thereafter he visited the village regularly. He mixed up with the villagers, asked them about their physical wellness, and gave them some necessary medicines. It was during such regular meetings that the topic of village development cropped up, and they made up their mind to develop the village. Chait Ram Pawar led them. First of all, they decided to protect the surrounding jungles. Though the forest department had employed guards for the job, but the guards seemed to be more cautious to secure and protect themselves rather than the forests. Chait Ram organised a committee in the village, which took subscription of ₹ 30/- per family per year, or in lieu, 7 kg *Nachani*, a light type of food grain. The committee appointed two village youths as choukidars to guard the jungle. These choukidars caught two persons red-handed when they were cutting bamboos illegally. They took them to forest department office, but no action was taken against the thieves due to their connivance with forest officer. So, the villagers imposed upon them a fine of ₹ 5000/-. Half of the money was sent to the forest department and the remaining half was deposited in the village account. There was no illegal cutting in the forest thereafter. *Mahua* trees, the trees that bear juicy yellow flowers used for preparing liquor, are assets and property. Liquor industry runs in every house, so the competitive rivalry, always, in collecting the *Mahua* flowers. The village committee, therefore, decided to auction the *Mahua* trees, and 102 *Mahua* trees were auctioned among the villagers. Thus, gradually, villagers developed love for the forests. The village prepares ropes also. Rope is made of a grass known as 'ghay pati'. Earlier the residents of Baripada used to go to other forests to fetch 'ghay pati', and that entailed disputes quite often. So the Chait Ram committee decided to grow 'ghay pati in their own forest. The forest department gave them saplings of 'ghay pati', and the forest of Baripada also started cultivation of the grass. Eucaliptus, bamboo and *gulmohar* were planted on the vacant land around the village. It was decided that each family will plant 110 plants. One hundred families contributed. Now there flourishes a new and glorious jungle of eleven thousand trees.

The work of Baripada attracted attention of government also. Government awards the villages noted for looking after forests carefully. Baripada got the reward of rupees fifty thousand. The villagers thought that the best use of that money would be to prepare jaggery. Their sugarcane yield was hardly purchased by the sugar mills, which hesitated to collect the sugarcane crops in their trucks from the faraway forest surrounded village. So the villagers decided to have their own factory, costing about rupees one and a half lakh, to make jaggery. Some machines were purchased with the rewarded money, and the remaining paraphernalia was arranged through subscriptions and *Shramdan*. Now Baripada crushes its sugarcane yield and prepares jaggery. Last year they produced 290 quintals of jaggery, and the village got the 'Van-Vyavasthapna' award again. That encouraged the villagers further.

Now there arose a dilemma. How to strike balance between meeting the requirement of fuelwood and saving forest. They deliberated and decided unanimously to allow wood cutting only for twenty days, and thereafter nobody would go to jungle for three months to have fuelwood. The newly-generated zeal in the villagers resulted in a new plan, named "Kisan Rop Vatika'. 'Rop' means plant. The forest department gave twenty-five thousand saplings to the village, to be planted, grown, and guarded by the village only. The villagers worked hard, honestly. In due course, they sold half of the plants to forest department. The remaining twelve and a half thousand were available for sale in market, but Chaita Ram proposed that the remaining plants should not be sold but distributed free of cost to nearby villages, as quite a good amount of payment had already been received from forest department. This proposal was accepted unanimously.

There are 104 families in Baripada. Unitedly, they guard their jungle. The village has a school with two lady teachers. A few years earlier, teachers came to the village only when some government official of education department visited the school. As a remedial measure, the villagers decided to impose a fine of ₹ 51/- on any absentee teacher for each day of illegitimate absence, and ₹ 1/- was the amount of fine on each absentee student, per day.

Now, both, teachers and students have set themselves right and become regular and punctual. The guardians too have understood the importance of education.

'Jan Sewa Foundation' is the name of a Pune-based institution. It provides guidance to farmers. Vanvasi Kalyan Ashram arranged a visit of agriculture expert Shri Dafedar to Baripada. He taught four formulae to farmers for getting good yield of paddy. They followed him, and there was remarkable increment in paddy production. Now they produce paddy on 80 hectares of land. They produce the *basmati* paddy, and R-420 also, not for sale, but for their own consumption. Kabaddi competition of Baripada is well known in the area. Kabaddi teams from other villages come to Baripada to play the game. The main aim of Chait Ram was not to hold Kabaddi competition, but to show the visiting teams the glorious attainments of Baripada. They were astonished to see the paddy farming in the village, and went back with new inspiration.

Chait Ram says that he invites some senior government officers for prize distribution after the kabaddi matches are over. We explain to them the development story of the village. They return with satisfaction, and we have come to know that many other villages have benefited from our experience. Of course, Chait Ram has become Chaitanya Ram.

□

"I know certain things that exist in you, which you may not be aware of at all. There is a great fountain of power in you, much bigger than what you deploy. There is unlimited stock of intellect in you, much greater than what you utilize. There are infinite capabilities in you for social service, much more than what you do for society."

—Adage

43

CHAMANLAL

Chamanlal passed away on February 11, 2003, at the ripe age of 83. It was a natural and age-related death, but everyone longed for his extended life span. I believe that one's death is more meaningful when people feel that he should have lived some more years, then death becomes more dignified. Chamanlal ji was rich in both, meaningfulness and dignity.

Who was Chamanlal ji? Most of the media-related people may not know him, because he never contested election, nor did he get any post that could make headlines. He was a *pracharak* of R.S.S., who had ascribed a sublime sense, and a highly auspicious meaning to the word *pracharak*. According to dictionaries, the word *pracharak* means a propagandist who propagates. To R.S.S. this limited definition of a *pracharak* is not acceptable. In R.S.S., *pracharak* means the person who has taken a pledge to be dedicated for the nation throughout life, rising above all worldly allurements, without any remuneration or honour, ever ready to go to a directed destination. It is such a person, who is a *pracharak* in R.S.S. A *pracharak* is not entitled for a '*Pranam*', a customary practice in a *Shakha* to accept salutation. However, he may be entitled for a '*Pranam'* if he is appointed in the line of *Sar Sanghchalak* or *Sar Karyavah*. He will stand in the line of ordinary *Swayamsevaks*. His attire will also be like an ordinary *Swayamsevak*. He does not wear any special dress. Though totally detached, a *Sanyasi,* he does not wear saffron robe. It is the innovation by the unique talents of Dr. Hedgewar, the founder of R.S.S., that a *pracharak*, though a *Sanyasi* in practice, and conduct, lives like a common man. Sant Jnaneshwar Maharaj, the renowned *yogi* saint of Maharashtra, has written about the behaviour of a learned man, "*Alaukika Nohave Lokanprati.*" It means that a learned person should not betray any impression of being unique, living with common people. That is how a *pracharak* lives.

Chamanlal became a *pracharak* after he earned M.Sc. degree with first position and a gold medal in the year 1942 in Lahore, which, unfortunately, is not with us now. Just imagine those days when a first class, gold medalist M.Sc. could achieve any appointment, at least a lecturership in a college, but Chamanlal ji chose to be a *pracharak*, and remained a *pracharak* for sixty years. One may raise a simple question, "What did he do as a *pracharak*?" The reply would be simple, "He did the Sangh *Kary*." There may be another question, "What does the Sangh *Kary* mean?" The reply would be, "Simple, holding *Shakha,* playing games, physical exercises, teaching 'dand' (stick), and singing songs."

Does someone dedicates ones life for only such activities? Yes, thousands have dedicated their life only for these activities. That is how R.S.S. has grown. Growth of *Sangh* means society is becoming stronger. A senior Army officer once asked Shri M.S. Golwalkar, affectionately addressed as Shri Guru ji, the second chief of R.S.S., "How do you motivate your *Swayamsevaks* so much that they are ever ready to stake their life for your cause, something our Army jawans may not do?" Shri Guru ji replied, "We teach them how to play kabaddi, and he learns that, but that is the kabaddi of Sangh style." How much did that officer understand from the reply may be difficult to say, but Shri Guru ji was right. The *Sangh* is built, grown, and growing day by day, because of practising the kabaddi-spirit.

Chamanlal ji was a *pracharak*, first in Mandi, then in Lahore, and after the Partition in Jalandhar. Thereafter, he was given the responsibility as office in-charge, which he carried on. Shri Madhav Rao Mule, the then *Prant pracharak* of Punjab, directed him to keep in touch with the *Swayamsevaks* who had gone abroad. He carried on that job also. He came in contact with Indians living abroad in many countries through the *Swayamsevaks*. His contacts in foreign countries resulted in the organisation named as *Vishwa Vibhag*, constituted by the *Swayamsevaks* of R.S.S. Chamanlal ji remains a foundation stone of the grand edifice of the *Vishwa Vibhag*.

A condolence meeting was convened on 16 February 2003 at the lawn of the R.S.S. office, Jhandewala, Delhi. People came from America, England, West Indies, Mauritius, Australia, Malaysia and Sri Lanka to pay homage to Chamanlal ji. Present in the meeting were the Vice-President of India, Shri Bhairon Singh Shekhawat, and the Deputy Prime Minister of India, Shri Lal Krishna Advani. The Prime Minister had attended the funeral procession and paid his tearful tributes to Chamanlal ji. It is not only the persons related with R.S.S., who paid him tributes. Lt. Gen (Retd.) Jacob, the Lt Governor of Punjab, Anerood Jugnauth, the Prime Minister of Mauritius, and Shri Krishna Moorthy, the former Election Commissioner, were not related with the R.S.S., but they were related with Chamanlal ji. They too paid warm tributes to him. He was not a politician. In his address, Vice-President, Shri Bhairon Singh Shekhawat gave a detailed account of how Chamanlal ji helped him when he (Bhairon Singh Shekhawat) had gone to America for surgery of his heart. His touching description brought tears in the eyes of many in the audience. The former Election Commissioner, Krishna Moorthy narrated how Chamanlal ji contacted him and enquired about his well being while he was in Sri Lanka during elections there. Chamanlal ji must have heard the Radio news of bomb explosions in Sri Lanka, so he contacted Krishna

Moorthy ji. Later on family members of Krishna Moorthy ji contacted Chamanlal ji over phone. It is impossible to count the number of the families having warm and cordial relations with Chamanlal ji. They were all overwhelmed with his closeness. In spite of his great popularity in society, he never allowed any feeling of conceit to enter his mind. "*Thou*" had replaced "*I*" in him completely. Editor of the then weekly Hindi magazine *Dharma Yuga* once asked Shri Guruji, "How would you describe the goal of your life in one sentence?" Shri Guru ji replied, "*Main naheen, too hee*" (not me, thou only). Chamanlal ji was an unexceptionally true follower of Shri Guru ji's '*Dhyeya Vakya*': Everything for Thou. This is the feeling of the '*Yajna*'. "*Agnaye Swaha*" (offering oblation to the God of fire) is not enough to complete the offering. One has to say, "*Agnaye Idam*", it has become for god of fire. Even then the offering is not complete. One has to say, "*Na Mama*", nothing of it is mine. Then only the offering is complete finally. The oblation of Chamanlal ji's life is an instance of such a perfect completion.

I came in contact with Chamanlal ji only three years back, though I knew him. He had grave concern about others, but not for himself. He washed his clothes himself, and never squeezed them, because, as he believed, life of the clothes is reduced by squeezing. Question of ironing his clothes never arose. It will not be an exaggeration to say that he was an epitome of politeness. While describing Sita ji poet Bhavabhuti says, "*Karunasya Moortisthava Shareerine.*" It means that Sita ji epitomises compassion. I would say about Chamanlal ji, "*Vinayasya Moortisthava Shareerine.*" Chamanlal ji epitomised humility.

It is said that once *Gopis* asked Krishna's *Murli* (flute) about its virtues that merited its placement on *Bhagwan* Shri Krishna's lips. The *Murli* gave a very touching reply:

"Pratham taj diyo sundar baans jhaaree ree,
Tana katavaayo, mana katavaayo,
Granthi – granthi men chhid karavayo,

Phir jaiso bajaawat hai Shyam,
Vaiso sur sunayo.
Yahi karan nij adharan par,
Rakhat Murari hai."
("प्रथम तज दियो सुंदर बाँस झाड़ी री,
तन कटवायो मन कटवायो,
ग्रंथि-ग्रंथि में छिद करवायो,
फिर जैसो बजावत है श्याम,
वैसो सुर सुनायो,
याही कारन निज अधरन पर राखत मुरारी है।")

The above confession of the flute may be translated into English language like this:

"First of all I renounced my beautiful bamboo bush,
Allowed my body and psyche
To be cut in pieces,
Suffered piercing,
On every pore of my body,
Then I sounded only the tunings played by Shri Krishna,
That is the reason why
Shri Krishna places me on his lips."

Shri Chamanlal ji transformed his life like a flute. He created resonance as played by the Sangh. Physical life of everyone has to end one day, but blessed is the life of those who spread uniquely sweet fragrance and supernatural intonations of their conduct. Chamanlal ji was one such great soul.

□□□

> *"So long as we love we serve; so long as we are loved by others, I would almost say that we are indispensable; and no man is useless while he has a friend."*
>
> **—Robert Louis Stevenson**